Living Colorful Beauty

by

Jonathan Harnisch

Living Colorful Beauty

Jonathan Harnisch

Babydude Press
36 Mariquita Lane
Corrales, New Mexico 87048
United States of America

ISBN-10: 1517786754

ISBN-13: 978-1517786755

CreateSpace Independent Publishing Platform, North Charleston, SC

Printed in the United States of America and Great Britain

Second Edition

Table of Contents

For the real Claudia...

INTRODUCTION

At the opening of *Living Colorful Beauty*, the reader is presented with two protagonists. There's Ben, the narrator of the preface, who relates the story of the awful sex education classes he sat through in middle school and of his subsequent discovery of his father's collection of pornography; and then there's Georgie, a sexual submissive with a foot fetish, who is obsessed with his beautiful and manipulative next-door neighbor Claudia. As the story progresses, however, it becomes clear that Georgie and Ben share a single three-dimensional body. Georgie is a character in a novel Ben is writing, and Ben maintains that Georgie is in fact no more than a literary device. However, it is clear almost immediately that this is not the case. Throughout his life, Ben has received a number of psychiatric diagnoses, ranging from Tourette's Syndrome to borderline personality disorder to schizoaffective disorder, and he displays some traits of all of these. Yet amid all these diagnoses, the one thing that seems to have slipped under the radar thus far is his tendency towards emotional dissociation, which is closely related to post-traumatic stress syndrome. It is this dissociative tendency that has led Ben to create Georgie, a safe repository for the emotions and desires – primarily sexual – that Ben himself is unable to process.

Initially, therefore, the life of Ben and Georgie is fairly well ordered. It is clear from the start that Ben has issues relating to women: his romantic life has been a string of broken relationships and missed opportunities, and though he needs love desperately he finds himself overcome by fear around women. Whenever this issue arises, Ben retreats into Georgie's relationship with Claudia. Claudia is compelling, manipulative, emotionally abusive, and tremendously sensual. She controls Georgie completely, only allowing him sex at certain times, alternately telling him she loves him and that she couldn't care less about him, telling him she won't sleep with him and then inviting him to watch her sleep with other men and other women. Yet Georgie is inextricably drawn to her, accepting all of the emotional pain that comes with his relationship with her as long as he can continue to hope that she may sleep with him again. The sex they share is gritty and fetish-laden, with strong overtones of sadomasochism and violence, and their relationship itself is sustained entirely by Georgie's obsession. Yet he is unable to let Claudia go. Similarly, Ben claims that Georgie's relationship with Claudia is based on his own relationship with Heidi – yet as the story progresses, we learn that Heidi is a lesbian whom Ben met once some months ago when she was in town for a conference, and that after one night, she left town and Ben had never heard from her again. In Ben's relationship with Heidi, mirrored in his imagining of Georgie's relationship with Claudia, it is clear that his interest is not in Heidi but rather in the image of Heidi, which, in the absence of the real Heidi, Ben can mold into whatever he needs her to be. Heidi is the locus of Ben's obsession, as Claudia is the locus of Georgie's; however, the root of these obsessive tendencies lies somewhere else entirely.

The root itself becomes clearer as Ben begins therapy with Dr. Christine Morales. Ben was initially put in therapy after a struggle with addiction issues and mania combined, which culminated in his attempting to hold up a bank with a cell phone he pretended was a bomb. Although Ben's participation in therapy was mandated by the police, Ben adapts to therapy quickly, beginning an honest attempt to learn the reasons for the addictions, disorders, and obsessions that are slowly killing him. Yet as soon as he begins to dig into these issues, he finds himself overwhelmed by the strong emotions and confusion that flood through him. It is clear that there is something that Ben can't bear to look at, something that has so shattered him that he has been forced to split his identity into two to keep himself feeling safe. He can't know what it is, but at the same time, his work in therapy causes him first to question and then to begin to dismantle the coping techniques he's developed – his alter ego Georgie, his addictions, his lusting after impossible women. He finds himself so conflicted that he goes off his medications entirely at one point, deliberately if subconsciously inducing psychosis to avoid having to face the terrifying question: *what it is that makes me act this way?*

When he returns to his medication and emerges from the psychosis, he realizes he can no longer avoid confronting the true issue. His mother has been a taboo subject for him all these years, his relationship with her a corner of his psyche he keeps securely closed down. With the help of Dr. C, he begins to process her abuse of him. He begins by relating the physical abuse she subjected him to then progresses to her emotionally abusive tendencies, but he is still strangely detached. Finally, on the brink of slipping once more into madness, he is able to remember the sexual abuse he suffered at her hands, the abuse that melded the concepts of arousal and repulsion in his brain, the abuse that left him yearning desperately for the love of a woman but unable to understand what healthy love might look like. With this knowledge, Ben can at last begin to confront his symptoms head-on and to hold out hope for a less troubled life.

Obsession is a state of mind,

So make it good!

...A PRELIMINARY REMARK:

Kelly doesn't know about my obsession with Claudia Nesbitt—or, rather, Georgie's obsession with her. I haven't told her much about the spells that haunt me either. I haven't mentioned a lot of things to her. I haven't mentioned how much I struggle to write anything original that comes from the heart. Or that all I hear is the chaos of the Devil and the angels, and the voice of Georgie dictating my every word and action. That I'm nothing but a trust fund baby with an addiction problem and a constellation of lurid sexual fetishes that shrink into petrified silence in the presence of any actual women and a half-dozen psychiatric diagnoses ranging from Tourette's syndrome to schizoaffective disorder.

. . . That I was taken into police custody for trying to rob a bank with nothing but a threateningly brandished cell phone and a reference to 9/11. That my father pulled some strings that landed me in rehab rather than prison. However, as part of one of the conditions of my release—that I must begin therapy with a court-appointed psychologist—I haven't really talked much about it. As I began to work in therapy, the issue that came into focus was that of Georgie, my alter ego, whom I'd conceived as living a parallel life to mine that mirrors and channels my own self-aware, yet foreign, emotional highs and lows.

. . . That with Dr. C's help and encouragement, and my own intelligence and determination—well, some determination and some pure laziness—I might peel away the layers of Georgie's existence, so that I might find the *determination* to hand over to Kelly all that I've kept inside, so she won't leave me, so that I can self-actualize and get over the bitch, Claudia, and be honest with her, with Kelly, and with myself . . . to meander out of some of the confusion. After all, sobriety has not cleared up all the fogginess; it seems to have added to it, seems to have created fucking stockpiles of it. And as the pieces of my existence have begun to emerge, they've done so with an extremely uncomfortable, agitating, transgressive, and self-loathing . . . *clarity*. The clarity is what's frightening me more than anything. In fact, I'm scared to fucking death of all this clarity.

0. PREFATORY

Looking back on it now, now that the words that come later can drain away most of the sentiment, there's a nostalgia that still lingers at the top of the Eiffel Tower, when *those kids*—three girls and two boys—defined who I was without the slightest hint of bias or negativity.

It was the first time in my life, the first "time of my life." I was on a school trip in Paris, with the same kids who would taunt me and bully me back in New York. And although I had forgiven them, even loved them to an extent, there was so much going on at home, and in my head, and in my body, that I couldn't tell the difference between what was good and what was bad, what was appropriate and what was not. Kids can be brutal.

They say that those in the "Losers' Clubs" in school will usually show up at the reunions, years later, as glittering icons, while the popular kids turn to waste. I never went to any of the reunions.

I took a left turn by not going with my class. I got permission from the French teacher who was in charge of us to hang out with another group of kids from another junior high school; they were also in Paris from Nassau County, and although I was away from my own crowd of popular kids (that particular crowd of waste), my new group of friends and I took off by métro that night after dinner. We climbed most of the Eiffel Tower, as it was still open to tourists, even at the late hour.

As we gazed over the city lights, the brisk wind blowing hard, one of the kids, Wesley, who couldn't have been over twelve—all wrapped up in his ski jacket, his short curly hair frozen, unaffected by the winds—smiled innocently to me, and as if it was his second nature, he said, coolly, "You seem pretty normal to me, Ben. Hey, you're one of us." And all the others bantered among themselves in agreement. I took a group photo of my new best friends, all of us arm-in-arm, holding on in the chill air, and holding on to the memory of being so free, without supervision. Looking back on everything now, the world, the universe, never looked as beautiful to me as it did during that cool breezy night on top of the world, where I was with my friends and nobody knew just how invincible we really were.

I haven't a clue what happened on the walk back to the hotel, and by the next day, when Wesley's and his buddies' vacation meant they'd be back in the States by sundown, I had forgotten about it. I mean I'd forgotten about everything—my introduction—and I went back to the in-crowd as they did what they did for the rest of the trip, mostly drinking French beer from the mini-bar in the Hôtel Chateau Martine.

I find that the more I keep to myself all that I do remember from that particular night out with the group from Paris, and as I wonder constantly if by now, they'd ever grown up or if they just stay the same, like in the picture I still have of them together. . . . It's under my bed, in an old shoebox—so that *I* can stay the same, somewhere, somehow . . . way deep down inside.

1. ROTTING IT OUT

You can see me close up, really close up. I'm here, stuck inside this little home office. Outside, it's scorching hot; I can barely breathe out there. Hell, I can barely breathe right in here anymore. I take my shirt off—it's a mail-order black T-shirt, says BITCH on the front in tiny white lower-case letters. It's drenched with sweat, a real sticky, pus-like kind of sweat—it fucking stinks, you know.

God, I'm all itchy, my whole fucking body itches, anywhere I've got the slightest tenderness to my skin—my ankles, inside my elbows, under my knees, my fucking groin, crotch, whatever—has scabs, flakes, growing from constantly scratching all these creepy-crawlies. I'm fucking grossed out, I'm so dirty, I'm just yucky, with ultra-blue-violet boils about to burst on my thighs—I can't close my legs right, it might pop the boils. Is it hep? Is it fucking AIDS? The doctors say it's not uncommon for a diabetic, like I am, to have these lesions, as I call them. In a way, I want AIDS, I want cancer—I want them so that I can go through more illness, so that I can overcome anything, maybe everything. Sort of rebelling, or conforming. I don't know. It's hard to do both at once.

The trees outside are losing their leaves, but the wilderness, the trees—everything is closing in, that's for sure. The tall trees block any view of the Sandia Mountains here in Albuquerque, and nature swallows up most of the irrigation water coming from the wishy-washy sludge of a creek they call the Rio Grande River. I can't see that either. Supposedly it's right down the street. Mosquitoes swarm all around, clit-nibbling my arms, my face, my ankles; it's a bee's nest, mosquitoes and wasps, fucking bugs out there. Can't run; can't hide from anything.

The walls here at home are concrete, cinderblock, '70s-stuff wood chips in the would-be flower pots, mulch lining the dry dirt-and-rock driveway—dirt (no grass) infested with goatheads and foxtails on the unmanicured lawn outside, like a run-down horse-hopping arena. I'm constantly irked, especially by the goatheads as they jam into my bare feet like sharp crystal glass—my stinky, dirty, overgrown, hairy, scarred, bare feet. Have to pull them off, each little fucking goathead, one by one, and the dogs keep bringing them in, too. The dogs, Rocko, Beaks, and Biscuit, without a doubt, have better lives than I, but they, too, wish the place here was better kept and that the weather wasn't too hot for them, or else they'd quit all the barking shit, all the time, barking at everything, but I've got to love them.

It's 120 goddamn degrees out there, not that the weatherman on Channel 4 will ever factor the humidity into the actual temperature—the humidity's up near 40%. So much for getting out of New York. So much for getting out of California. So much for this suffocating morsel of love, living in his living hell—the morsel of a man that I call myself.

I've set up all five of my video cameras (plus the two Super-8s for show, but they won't record automatically)—they're all pointed at me in here. Zoom out a little, and you'll see the scattered papers, old dried-out pens, spittoons for my smokeless tobacco, overflowing ashtrays, fucking ciggies on the floor, ground into the already-burnt and bland off-tan carpet—hotel-chain-style, public-domain décor. Got a finished dinner plate in my hand that I've lowered to meet the constant gaze of one of the terriers; it's just got some yellow egg yolk smeared on it, but Rocko enjoys the taste of just about anything. Except, of course, his own recalled-last-week, and his last-year-as-well, generic pet food from the Emporium.

We've got help here—staff, what-have-you—so it's not like I'd even prepared this morning's breakfast myself. Everything's kind of done for me. It was all that Kelly and I could do for ourselves to get help now that the rest of my trust fund has been cut off by my father, Martin Schreiber, who insists that I live by his principles—which for the moment consist solely of the command that I "shall commit myself" to terminal hospitalization, which I don't need . . . Telling me I've got borderline personality disorder is a bit ironic, as it would imply that he caused it himself, as my abandoning parent. On the same side of the coin, any psych hospital should be effective enough in helping me to recognize that most of my current issues are the result of his malicious, violent, sexually, and even emotionally abusive relationship with me, which went on for years. This shit-face is entirely in denial—or something. I should hire a hit man

20

to shoot him in the face, and bill it to him. After all, I've been cut off financially by him; he's committed fraud with my tax forms, fucking signing my name numerous times on legal documents, trying to get me audited or something. I've given Pops my share of hell, too. But who cares? I did what I did to him out of spite, and because I love him.

I look into the cameras, one by one: Remember me? Remember that old aluminum baseball bat I kept on my wall for show? You used to clobber me on the head with it. Remember? You really tried. Didn't know any better way, any alternative. I remember once, just after the Little League game. You failed to make it to the game at all, you said you had work to do. You waited for me back home, and I was terrified of you. That was then, I shouldn't complain now. I shouldn't complain . . . ever. I'll laugh it off later. Please accept my apologies. I was wrong and inappropriate. It won't happen again, I promise.

Remember when you asked me to "come in and see" when I caught you and that hideous street hooker snowballing on your nuts, and you told me, "It's cool; just don't tell your mother." That it was "guy stuff"? You were in heaven, Pops; sure I'd never seen you so vulnerable as you were that night. You'd have done anything for that whore. What ever happened to her?

#

Martin's gold-digger, picture-perfect wife (the Life Coach, the Family Philanthropist, the Saint of Google Searches, Living Colorful Black-Dahlia-Wanna-Be) requires that I live by the principles set forth in her all-time-favorite self-help book, *The Four Agreements*. If I don't conform to these, Gladice will make my "life a living hell," she says—not that it isn't already. That's what she writes to me, that's what she brags to her pompous army of control victim confidantes; that is, that once my father passes away, she'll turn into this feminist Hitler—this dictator of brainwashed children. She longs passionately for what her poon provides her. Distance and boundary marks—F-ing stench, the taste of her living colorful salt, a patch of gray on her pussy. Gladice's own living colorful chaos, of havoc, of frustration with her marriage resulting with her typical American womanly whining and hissing and crying; I can't stand it.

"I should have been president," is what she'll sink down to and remember, "but you guys, this family really fucked it up for me! *Whaaah!*" I'll make love with her entangled strands of clump, of hair, of her pubic pie; in this sick fantasy, she has me wear a rubber because that's just good practice. Besides, I don't want a kid who's more fucked up—mentally and physically—than I am. No need to replace my scapegoat status. Don't want another fucking case study like me. I tell all this stuff to the cameras, in case they ever need the *cause of death—my* cause of death. That's if anyone should ever come to think about actually accessing the tapes, if anyone ever cared.

The cameras are a way for me to control the paranoia.

#

I'm going to die in four years. Not one year, and not five years—and not twenty-five or even fifty years. I don't know how I know this; I just believe it. It just kind of came to me one day—kinda came to me like a hunch, you know.

I don't have much of a life anymore. I know it's not good to ramble and talk and write about depressing things or about the past—two no-nos. But that's my plan. Sound like a plan? Well, no, it doesn't sound like *anything*—it's just probably what's gonna happen. And I'll stick a lotta non sequiturs and utilize some wit in crafting the individual sentences, and who knows, they might even border on brilliant. It's what I know, and it's what I'm good at; it's what I'm best at. And nobody else can be better at what I do best, specifically. It's important for me to realize that. Spiritualism Is King.

#

I'm stiff. My bones and muscles are stiff and fragile. Can't reach to put on my socks or even my left pant leg, much less do any washing of my feet in the shower. I can't even dry off right. Kelly helps me with that.

I met Kelly about a year ago online. She was editing two of my screenplays—both of a romantic nature, mostly basically plagiarized anyway—and I began to flirt with her through the bulletin board of the editors' main website, until I received that personal e-mail in my personal inbox—the e-mail that let me know that "the fish was hooked."

I managed to stay alert enough in my debilitation to keep Kelly interested in me and what I "had" to offer. Eventually we moved in together—in Long Beach, California—and then I let my sickness take over again; then I moved down to Albuquerque, where Kelly had her life as it was before and she could navigate the town and all. I'd been burning bridges in LA as it was anyway, and things were not working out for me out there any longer—again, as it was; as it was not. Period.

Now, about what I want. I mean, as in what I want as the main character in my own novel—this one—*Living Colorful Beauty* . . . Well, that sort of changes. Sort of like in *Good Will Hunting*. Will, at first, wants to hang out with his roughneck buddies, then he wants that Skylar chick, then he doesn't know what he wants (to be a shepherd?), then he wants to work with the NSA. But then he goes after Skylar, again, at last, and the movie ends. Hollywood ending. Academy Award. You could say Will Hunting wanted to self-actualize, overall. And, in a big way, that's what I want. I want to put it out there so there is little confusion, as this book has already proved to be a plot-less work of chaos. I want to find out about Georgie, and to end my obsession with Claudia—or maybe not. No, maybe not, I think, no. And I want to be able to love, to know what love is and how to love while not just having sex, not just fucking women. Fucking, I want something good to last, yes, yes, and yes, I want a normal, loving relationship. I want to be loved, and to manifest all of this in my real personal life—just like most of the story thus far, which has been written, sort of shows me, Ben, living full-time in his obsessions and fantasies, which is entirely the case.

I want to work it out with Kelly long-term, and before she leaves me like everybody else has—like pretty much all my friends and all my family, who've fucking left me to raise myself, by myself, and to live all by my own shitty-assed self. Fuck them! That's it, I'm angry. FUCK THEM. And SO FUCKING WHAT.

#

Dr. C agrees with Kelly that it's probably a good idea to write out some more of the gross stuff, the violent and sexual stuff—maybe not in that order, maybe the sexual stuff first. Doc C asked me just yesterday about what specifically it was that I was talking about that I wasn't willing to write about. I explained it to her. "For example, the way, how salty my stepmother's pussy tastes." How about that?

Doc C looked concerned, slightly cautious, and said, "Yes, I would ask you to write that kind of stuff down, true or untrue." Then she went on to say how much she hates the stuff that Hollywood's coming out with—and that she's not one, herself, who cares much for any 'story arc,' or any inventive 'through line' or any happy 'wedding endings.' The 'real' kind of stuff, even depressing plots, tend to find her better entertained, better 'brained,' make her feel her time was better spent.

I agreed with Dr. C. I said, "Dude, man, I know."

I did feel inclined to just be myself all morning, not to get up or get going, but I felt too forced to act as I was dragged out of bed and into the morning routine stuff by Kelly. Kelly's got this strong desire to 'help' me and to get the 'old me' back, to have her true 'partner' back—it comes out in her frustration 'with the world in general.' I don't believe her. I think it's me, I think she gets 'mad' at me; I tell her this, and she says, 'not mad, just frustrated,' and I tell her, 'Same thing, you know what I mean, mad or frustrated, same thing.' I'm trying my best to simply get up with her, get in the shower, take my meds, and take an active role in 'our' mornings—I try not to lie on the couch all morning when she's all active and productive-like, unlike me with my smokeless tobacco lodged in my lower lip—but it's hard, really fucking hard. It's good that Kelly and I have in-home care coming now, and now more often than last week, when they first came to the house—they came, initially, to distill all of Kelly's worries and insecurities, although only some, not all, of Kelly's insecurities and worries could be quelled at once. In fact, she's been a real trooper with me. I have no clue how difficult her living with me has been and how unending the stress and frustration have been for her—it takes a noticeable toll on her. She won't really s█████But for the most part she's tending to my every need, because my health is important to her; we just might find some peace and some kind of happiness, whether together or apart, in the long run.

Georgie always says that, in the long run, I'll be fine. Georgie comes and goes, but he's always been a part of me. More than just a part, he's a Seraphim angel—like Michael, Gabriel, even Lucifer before he fell, maybe even after falling. I haven't figured out all that much about him. Sometimes he manifests in my life like the Devil, instilling chaos, fucking with my electronics, and scaring the cats away here at home. Other times, he is Seraphim, the angel. Apart from that, he's otherwise a part of me, as we move ahead, as we back-step; he's kind of always there in the foreground with me as I offer him my confessionary details, my sins, my fetishes—even scat and incest. I know it can get pretty bad, pretty crazy, pretty sick—and I perhaps selfishly hand over whatever insecurities I have to Georgie. He's more of the passive type, a passive observer, even as I observe and judge him, but since he's stickier than I am— yes, he is sticky and jelly-like, blob-like, but fresh, not foreign— I have an easier time passing my symptoms and pathologies onto him. It's almost as if he doesn't mind.

Sometimes we will fight about things, usually when I'm off my psychotropic medication for a period of time or when I just get so fed up with my life experiences that wanting to attempt a fucking crime is not a safe possibility; those are the times when I figure I can dissociate when I'm overwhelmed and fantasize with Georgie. Letting go—well, I have hardly any social life at this point in my life, and no 'real-world' experiences in which I participate, so yes, I'm pretty much bound to whatever place I'm in and with whom I'm with. Divine intervention tends to offer me whichever place and time I'm involved in at the moment. The people I'm with come partly from my giving all other people I know all the control over my life that I can. I'm trying to sell my life, giving money away, for example, lots of money, fucking lots, to anyone who might trade it for my sanity, tranquility, fulfilled hope, lessened fears . . . some kind of love, whatever that is.

My family is fucking crazy—the whole extended and nuclear family—the Living Colorful "Rich." Erratic boundaries, even sexual boundaries, neglect . . . the same stuff you hear about everybody else in America. You know, they have a really high rate of medical cures in Third World countries, and families there tend to hold together well. I live a couple of hours from Mexico, basically. Must be a good sign. Never get that fucking family to feel my love once I arrive in Barbados; I can't feel their love for me—love is the Satanic cult I've disengaged from, from when they'd forgive me for being myself while I worshipped them—they swung around the metal can of sulfur smoke, they loved me all my life. They navigate my angels and demons; they revive me. I say, fuck them. I say that because I did. I hope I don't bring any of that up again. Most of that stuff, I'll need to keep to myself, just so that I've got some secret for myself, so that I can feel like I have something—generally speaking. I've done the incestuous gig. I've fucking been there, too.

Although I won't read anything they might send me, and I never answer the phone anymore, anyway, especially if it's Pops, my father's still trying to buy this house so that I 'can live here rent-free.' He wants to buy my dream house; he's already bought my other dreams, and so has my stepmother, Gladice. *She* started a small publishing company when she found out that I wanted to start one myself. *He* started funding films and film festivals when he knew I wanted a film career. They said I'd never have to work and that I shouldn't work, and now I know why, it's because they wanted to buy me out and control me—now they want to kidnap me and knock me unconscious and fly me on the private jet to a mental institution and long-term rehab, even though I've been sober for over five years now. The transgression is lovely.

I was going to go and read what I've just jotted down for Kelly to see if I'm on the right track again, but she seems to be in another one of her frustrating moods, must have just received another crappy e-mail from someone in my family—probably Gladice—because instead of going to bug her in her office, I had a smoke just outside her office, her windows opened, and I could hear she was on the phone with one of her lawyer friends, asking about my father and my trust fund. I know she feels insecure and really feels she deserves long-term benefits, and my family's trust and appreciation, too. But I'll tell ya, she ain't goon a get any of that shit from Ben's family, the fuckers.

Kelly needs to cum, but she hasn't let me near her coot in a long while. I feel like jerking off to one of the tit-pics I have of the late transgressive writer Kathy Acker—she reminds me of Claudia, but Claudia's tall, maybe five foot ten—I love jerking one, once in a while for Kathy Acker, even with her double mastectomy and stretch marks. She's nice, I'll say. I like nice. I can deal with nice and cool. Good fantasy. Good feeling. Nice.

In doing so, I train my hand for war, for pointing my finger against myself and feeling everybody else, as my heart seems to have gone astray and into a subsequent intermission of a delicate obsession with someone Georgie calls Claudia. Things started back when we were invincible, when we were young, when we were kids, when we were curious. We had nothing else that was good enough to last. Something we could really hang onto.

I wonder if Kelly knows about all the longing I've felt, just to . . . just to . . . be alone. Just to exist. To be . . . anything, even nothing. Sixth grade was an acid trip, straight out of a summer movie, or something:

2. SECOND SKINS

I used to get mad at my school
The teachers that taught me weren't cool

—The Beatles

"Class," Mrs. Petite said, "today is our first day of sex education."

We snickered. We were in sixth grade. Of course we snickered.

Mrs. Petite frowned, the lines across her forehead deepening. Her voice became clipped. "Before we begin, everyone present in this class will be required to say aloud the following words, without any laughter: Sex. Penis. Vagina. Breasts."

"Say, 'Sex,'" she told us.

"Sex," we said.

"Okay, class, good. Georgie, especially good."

From Mrs. Petite, I heard for the first time the very words I would come to know so well as an adult. I never even hinted at a smile as I continued . . .

"Penis. Vagina. Breasts."

Dick. Pussy. Tits . . . Cock. Cunt. Noonies.

Twenty years later, the latter part of "breasts" still whistles through my teeth as I struggle to make it plural.

"Breast-ts-ts-ts."[1]

Back in class.

"Always use a condom," Mrs. Petite said.

"Always use a condom . . ." the class repeated in unison.

I will never forget: Always use a condom.[2]

---

[1] Lunch Break/Recess: Sex Ed seemed to go on forever. I sat on the sidelines of the girls vs. boys kickball game and told this other kid about my mother beating me and how rich I was going to be. We ate at Bennigan's just about every night, sometimes Red Lobster—my mother served very large portions and burned her food when we ate at home. Our house was a pigsty.

"You like Dungeons & Dragons?" this kid asked me.

"Mmm, no."

I collected my first porn when I was nine, pilfered from my father's closet. Nothing nice. Nothing tame. No *Playboy*. No *Penthouse*. Straight to *Taboo, Cherry Poppers*. A sticky, dog-eared copy of *Anal Amateurs*.

At ten, I was more than determined to actually purchase my first X-rated magazine, all by myself, using a portion of the Christmas money I had saved up from my Aunt Beatrice.[3]

---

[2] I'll never forget how I liked Mrs. Petite 'cause I would fantasize about her mature naked skin and her husband, who came to class once. How I wanted to take her from him. Like Pops took Inball Schneider, office porn delight, or Letty Kremlin, super writer, super intimidating, perfect person, no flaws. Honest, no flaws. A great wife, into love, not money, not my cup of tea, my bowl of coal—Letty, Letty—I want you, not. I want to see the world through your eyes. Skinny dip with you, and nibble on your chlorine-painted ears. Letty, you make my fat feel good. (I said that to someone before, but after the words meant less, more or less. I sunk into something psychotic. I became an episode. Of reruns. Of ass and honesty . . . and smut-love, no he didn't, he's a serial killer, a rape victim, a son . . .)

[3] *Crazy Aunt B . . .* a short woman with her couple of unwanted curves, short, spiked gray hair with her assertive, tight-lipped Frenchman's face; a woman who could and would talk her fucking head off, in her own Brooklyn-Queens accent, about anything at all. She'd usually bring her opinions, or judgments, down to the same argument, would pout. "Oh, what these kids are up to these days, I swear. . . ." Eventually she'd turn her argument toward me: "*Georgie, you bedda learn, you bedda learn, kiddo.*"

I grew up surrounded by people like this, people I couldn't stand, people who would judge me even if I'd judged them to myself. And yes, I felt judged by Aunt B . . . after all, I wasn't a jaundiced vegan like she was, nor was I a follower of the rules of her house ("don't touch anything and no snooping") during Christmastime or during Thanksgiving dinner ("take it and eat it or leave it, *you bedda learn, you bedda.*") I was usually skipping dinner entirely, learning, looking up my cousins' skirts, flirting with them as if they weren't blood but schoolmates. We were playing my own somewhat secret version of Hide & Seek with the family kids and with friends of the family—the Puberty Edition of medical games like Operation, or even our own, tamer games like Show & Tell—Home Edition (Triple-X), games that I would lead by involving cousins and sisters, even the older ones, sometimes. I had a thing for the older ones, the ones with slogans like 'BOYS' ironed on their teenybopper T-shirts—

Anyway, one day I ditched recess and the elementary school itself. Instead of playing kickball or Asses Up with the other kids, I rode my BMX to the Quik Fix on Maple and Fourth. Stepping inside, I saw the place was surely empty of other customers and that nobody too imposing was working at the counter. It turned out to be Randy, with his acne scars and his sixteen-year-old "I don't give a shit" posture, the most promising, for me, of all the employees I'd ever seen work there. Funny, he wasn't in school either. He sat behind the counter.

"Hey man," I said, cool, and I continued to tell him I was eighteen and that I was there to buy a magazine.

"*Hustler*," I told him.

"Yeah, right," he said, his breath hitting my face; it was rank, stank of coffee and cigarettes, and I pulled back.

"Tell you what," Randy said, a smug smile on his face. "If you can reach *Hustler*, you can buy it."

I couldn't reach *Hustler*, but I could easily reach *Genesis*, and it was mine, just like Randy promised. I paid for it, then rolled it up, stuck it down the front pocket of my jeans and pedaled back to school in time for class.

#

A year later, the three of us—Lonnie, Andrew, and me—organized a sex club, a kiddie brothel. We set it up inside the built-by-Boy-Scouts tree house (thanks to Lonnie's two older brothers, our main benefactors) in the backyard. We played tame, safe games there, like Truth or Dare, Truth or Double Dare, and Spin the Bottle. We played nasty, kinky games, got the girls to act out the scenes from our forbidden stacks of magazine layouts and videotapes.

Several girls—our age and younger—let us finger-fuck them. They *made* us taste their bubble gum cum off our dipping fingers. We called it "hitting third base," then we hit second next, took first last. We liked going backwards like that—starting at

anything they did with me seemed a little forbidden, like they weren't *supposed* to be teasing with us kiddos.

Besides, X-rated photographs never judged me. I could look at them for hours on end, and think . . . *everything*.

third, working our way back to something tame. Once we'd "made out" with each other, we were officially "going out."

We had a pee-pail up there and we watched Kathy Friedlander, the girl I was going out with, pee with little effort, and then she wanted to watch me. I had asparagus for dinner, probably every night, for that matter, so I gladly took Kathy in private to the bathroom downstairs in our house, near the garage. I sat down to pee. I knew that the asparagus would cause my pee to smell funny. But Kathy wasn't too thrilled.

"No," Kathy said, "you don't make pee-pee sitting down. Stand up so I can see."

I told her I couldn't see crap when *she* was sitting down, well, squatting over the flower pot up in the tree house, but hell, I stood up anyway and soon lost all fear of my semi-public pee. We made out and ended up fucking through high school, but we didn't tell a soul, because she was unpopular and I was a fucking computer geek, Math League contestant, fucking teacher's pet. It was like we had adult minds, trapped in our little-kid costumes. It all started at our little wilderness, our secluded clubhouse where porno was preferred to pussyfootin'. I did other things those years, too, stuff for school and sports and shit, and I knew I had many talents.

These days, I look back on those times when we were all invincible. Our fathers, brothers, and cousins never knew where their stacks of *Playboy* and *Penthouse* had disappeared to. We knew exactly how to access them, like we were at the library, we only borrowed them, and the clubhouse remained full of variety and bulk material.

And latex condoms. We kept it safe. We kept it real.

The next year, when I was in seventh grade, my father dropped a box of non-lubed rubbers on my bed. I thought he'd discovered our little sex club in the backyard and was encouraging me. He wasn't.

"Always use a condom, Georgie. Double up if you have to," Pops reminded me so candidly. "I left a lifetime supply in your bedroom. They're pretty self-explanatory."

"Huh?" I said, embarrassed. I was ten.

"What's your business is your business," he said, "just use them and use them well."

"Don't worry, Pops, I will."

"No babies and none of that hokey pokey stuff, ya hear?"

"Of course, Pops, I know."

I opened a couple of samples of the latex condoms as well as *Webster's Dictionary*. I knew we could have a better supply for the tree house at our fingertips, but I decided to keep these for myself. It was time for research.

la·tex - a milky liquid or usually white sap in certain plants, such as the poinsettia . . .

con·dom - a thin sheath, usually of rubber . . .

Whatever the fabric was called, however it was defined in a book—rubber, latex, plastic, lambskin—I enjoyed feeling the complete covering of my private part; that smooth baby soft "sheath" was like heaven to me. It reminded me of those fascinating stress squeezer balls you find in novelty gift shops, or the substance that filled the inside of that elastic-y action figure—Stretch Armstrong.

As an adult, I pleasured myself with the latex wrapped around me—snug, warm, wet with saliva. There was no mess to clean up when I was through.

#

That's right, I think, as the saliva of other women and their vaginal juices complement my less frequent sexual experiences later on in my thirties. I invite any woman who has a fetish for latex herself to share that desire with me. Her looks don't matter all that much. Something can always be done about that. I have a lot to cover up myself and what I need is a partner with enough dignity to cover up all her flaws with a second skin. I have issues in my adult life, a fear of getting somebody pregnant. I fear big responsibilities since I wasn't brought up with any.

Looking back, all my sexual preferences seem to have been selected with such divinity and with a sense of appropriateness: older women who already have kids or can't have kids or don't mind the balloon around my dong, even better if they prefer it; a woman who doesn't want kids; a clean woman; a safe woman—but a wild party is always welcome, especially if she makes the first move and happens to live right next door. Someone with issues.

Someone like Claudia, who loves latex, but not on her lover, only on herself.

Claudia Nesbitt must have been the daughter of a 1960s feminist who taught her to hate men.

She wanted me to suffer and used her limited charms to lure the bottom-feeding, desperate, love-starved men of our culture, men like myself, into her web. Regardless of how susceptible I was to her seductive temptations, Claudia cast me as a victim of conspiracy.

What happened? I was such a good little kid.

But how I overcame Claudia's trap safely is what matters the most. I'm freed from her at last, and the real me was uncovered through the discovery of the real her.

Claudia had a thrilling personality, always upbeat and perky. She spoke in short sentences that got right to the point. Her otherwise pale face was decorated with glitter, like an adolescent princess, and her arms were covered with temporary tattoos of the Lucky Charms marshmallows.

Claudia lived for Harley Davidsons, had never owned one but dated guys who did. She dated a lot of guys. Her favorite pastime was Six Flags Magic Mountain or Six Flags Over Texas or Six Flags Over Georgia. Mostly, though, it was Six Flags Magic Mountain. Vintage wooden roller coasters satisfied her lust for things fast and chaotic, and then there were the dangerous affairs, hard liquor, pot laced with angel dust, and the occasional visit to King Arthur's strip club in the Valley with the women who swooned over her.

She never paid for a thing. She had herself to offer, and her package always seemed plentiful—those naturally luscious lips others would pay thousands to own and her oversized, natural pear-shaped breasts, the form of which I could discern only by the stretch and pull of the second skins that covered them.

Across the street, her original handwritten diaries detailing her adult sex life were placed open on the living room coffee table, along with a closeted collection of toys, costumes, and a wardrobe of textiles throughout the rest of her house. Her favorite apparel was a blue latex jumpsuit with fluorescent-green latex boots, along with a matching two-inch-thick green belt with an orange buckle, black gloves, and a black cloak. It spelled C-O-V-E-R M-E U-P, all of me.

Claudia was the type of naughty next-door neighbor you'd find in your favorite wet dream. She had a slightly sagging ass, but it sagged in just the right sexy way, like a real woman's. I stared at it when she stepped out for the mail in her terrycloth bathrobe and just-washed wet hair. She'd answer the doorbell in skimpy latex lingerie, oftentimes just a smooth rubber bra or black electrical tape crisscrossing her relaxed puffy nipples. She sucked fire out of the mailman's breath any time there was a special delivery that wouldn't fit in the mailbox. She illuminated temptation.

Otherwise, she was rather quiet and subdued, a secret control freak. Her visual cues and her charms exaggerated the mind's ability to make fantasies perfect. She'd fall asleep in her first-story bedroom with the blinds open, a nightlight on the wall and glow-in-the-dark stickers of the stars and planets on the ceiling. She lived alone and often woke up for a midnight snack. I watched her. Her refrigerator was covered with pictures of herself, all self-shot. In some, she was sticking her tongue out, and in others she just showed off her paint-covered feet or an obscure angle of what I figured was her vast beige areola. The cockpits of her nipples had wrinkles and folds that got geometrically complex when she was aroused, even slightly.

Unfortunately, those were only pictures of the real thing.

What could she be hiding? I often wondered. Never was she to be seen in her naked element. All to be mine, some day, but then again perhaps never mine.

Anyone who has the benefit of experiencing Claudia would love to hate her, unless they enjoy deception. She is a manipulative she-devil in disguise. Her Jekyll comes out when she wears a second skin to cover up her all-too-sinful nature and prize-winning ethics.

She was drenched with forbidden qualities, but as the puny, pathetic, desperate, wimpy horndog across the street from her, I was attracted to Ms. Nesbitt because I could directly correlate, from each piece of her puzzle, things that I once enjoyed or things that I could never have, the forbidden kinds of things that I just didn't have the balls for. Besides, we both had a thing for fabric.

Claudia seemed, at least at first, the complete antithesis of my mother, who was strict and abusive. Since my mother had learned things the hard way, by force, so would I. She, like my schoolteachers, taught me to be faithful, to practice safe sex, not to be gay or sexually ambiguous, and to be normal, whatever the hell that meant.

"Act like a human being," my mother would holler at me. "You look like a damn zombie half the time, Georgie. Fucking smile! Be excited."

"You're obsessed with sex! Don't dwell on sex," she'd constantly demand, slapping me across the face or screaming over the telephone. She found out about our sex club in the tree house by the time I left home for boarding school, when she had to take the smut posters off the walls herself.

"Don't do drugs. Don't drink. Don't cheat. Don't pretend. Don't worry about everything all the time."

All these learning experiences . . . Jeez!

Partway through my college years at NYU, I started to see a shrink, some proper, sweater-wearing old lady doctor who gave me the creeps and who, if possible, was even more controlling and critical than my mother was. Dr. Jenny Danielson. Dr. Jenny was certain that I had a lot of letting go to do. She said I wore a mask over my face. Literally: my goatee and mirrored shades, she said, they hid me. She'd tell me, "Take them off and shave your beard. Let me see the real you."

But I never did.

Claudia, on the other hand, was a perfect match for me. We were two doomed, tortured souls. She had many relationships, gay and straight, even married men and married women. She said she questioned her affairs, but since they made her feel good she held onto them. Claudia did drugs. I didn't. I'd had a problem with drugs and quit. Claudia didn't think she had problem with much of anything and never quit. I had to run five miles a day to just barely keep in shape. Claudia didn't have to work out, and still she maintained a perfect body. She was poor, and I was rich and thought I could spoil her. Claudia practiced unsafe sex. I preferred rubbers. She was forty. I was thirty. She was a ball of chaos. She was a marriage counselor who'd never been married, a parenting educator who'd never had kids, a rehab counselor who'd never been rehabbed herself.

But what bothers me most about Claudia Nesbitt is that once she lured me in, anytime I would call her, or want to see her, or fuck her with a rubber, I would have to wait far longer than my cock could bear. I was continually let down. I wasn't allowed to make out with her in the middle of our street because her girlfriend might show up any minute. She would swap spit with married men right on the sidewalk by my kitchen window, but she'd rarely reciprocate with me. She couldn't love me. I knew it. Yet when she did, when it seemed she did, those rare moments were holy and divine.

She was, and is, a no-win situation, but when Claudia got into her latex gear and refused any rubber with me, she was simply incredible. I couldn't, I can't, get her out of my mind. I loved her beyond my dignity, became sensually (or rather sexually) obsessed with her, and was dying to see her naked. As a masochist, I was in the perfect relationship. I loved everything about her and could never have a healthy relationship with her. Everything was strained, and as I became obsessed with the agony she caused in me, my character deteriorated. I became a much less dignified person as time went on.

I started to not even like myself much.

The last night we were intimate, about a month after the time before, we proved to be inseparable until our second skins came off. Just when I thought I'd had enough torture and emotional abuse from Claudia Nesbitt, I discovered a small handwritten note by my front porch. "Find your costume and just show up. Your unexpected entrance last month was morning bliss . . . until today. Having not seen you in some time, my affection toward you has cooled down to mere fondness. I'm becoming indifferent. I don't want that. We're separated from each other far too often, you live right next door."

I gasped, chewing a bite of one of the homemade oatmeal cookies she left with the letter. I continued to read:

"So, Georgie, as you know, since my house was robbed last week, I have no products left in any of the closets. It must have been some pervert who ripped off my skins and toys. But I've changed since then. Come over and see for yourself. I'm sorry for otherwise completely amputating myself from your life. I didn't have time. I require you, tonight."

Immediately, I grabbed my orange jail jumpsuit from last Halloween—I was an escaped convict—and I stormed over to her place with the cloth and cuffs in my hands. A box of rubbers was clenched between my teeth as I ran across the street. I was in such a hurry for love, lust, and submission that I left the keys to the handcuffs in the bedroom closet along with my unmentionables. I wasn't sure if we would need the keys anyway. I didn't know what to expect. Claudia in the flesh?

#

The door slammed shut behind me.

"No condom tonight, baby boy!" her voice called out from the bathroom. "Throw them in the fireplace before I come out."

I kept a couple in my pocket and dropped the box into the blaze. Claudia stepped out, fully nude, to watch the sizzling of the cardboard as it disappeared in the fire.

"The fire that keeps your house warm might eventually burn it down," she said seductively.

I gazed at her pale flesh.

"You changed," I said. "You're . . . perfect."

"I'm doing the best that I can," she sang quietly, in her best Beatles voice.

There were no drugs, no other lovers present, no tattoos, no secret diaries, and no make-up, not even any jewelry.

Finally Claudia was nude, completely nude. She had not one little blemish on her skin to ponder. There should have been music playing to the gentle beats of her all-natural, angelic presence. No sooner did this idea come to mind than she turned on the CD player.

It must have been one of her Beatles days.

> *Woman, I know you understand*
> *The little child inside of the man*
>
> —John Lennon

She played The Beatles all day long when she was in her most pleasant moods, taking care of spring cleaning across the way. Now I was with her again, for our final sexual experience together. I had waited so long for this.

The window shades were closed. We were sharing a private wilderness.

Claudia lit a few beeswax candles and pushed the coffee table over to the side of the living room. Cautiously, she bent herself over and covered her eyes, spreading herself wide open, gaping for me. The abstract pulp of her pussy was tucked snug beneath her dark pubic Hitler 'stache.

What in the hell was this woman thinking?

I paused. Claudia started dripping ever so slightly onto the hard wooden floor.

I'd been erect for about five minutes. I rolled down my shorts. I decided to double up in secrecy, fearing the worst.

Watching her loose lips dangle like the beads of a pearl necklace, loose, free, and liberated, I entered my covered key into her flesh machine, the forbidden gates of a hell I'd never seen before. I just didn't know it then.

The smell of perfume seemed to vaporize throughout the room. The sound of moist suction had the fibers in my mind vibrating until any sense of control was lost.

"Harder," she cried.

I fucked her harder.

"Deeper," she said. "Don't stop, Georgie."

The condoms were on, and she didn't notice.

"I'm so wet," she cried again. "I'm so wet because of you."

More fleshy friction made the sounds of a sensual circus. I reached around and indexed her erect little clit.

"The clit is so important, sooo sensitive," Claudia moaned. "Put your spit on it, hurry."

I did and reached back around and underneath. I rubbed her swell in small circles with two fingers, then three. I massaged her pronounced outer labia back and forth as it twitched. She was throbbing quicker than the beats to John and Yoko's *Double Fantasy* album that was still on repeat, track ten, "Woman." The taste of grapes dipped in corn syrup, that's all I could think.

I was about to erupt but held it as long as I could.

"I'm so close, Georgie," Claudia revealed. "I love you, baby. I fucking love you."

Suddenly, at the point of no return, both of my rubbers snapped open at once. We could both hear a light, defeating clicking sound. The first break was followed immediately by the second at the moment I let my sperm through to her haven, earlier than usual.

Claudia's personality shifted instantly. She became her old self once again.

"Oh, great." She sighed.

I carried myself off her, rising to the balls of my feet and squinting down at the floor.

"I think something popped," she said, as if she were glad it had happened. "I think you doubled up on the pleasure I asked you to get rid of."

I couldn't speak a word. I was shattered in a million pieces. All my dignity was lost.

"Are you on the pill, Claudia? Please say yes."

She shook her head 'no' and smiled slightly.

I remembered the time I'd told her I never wanted to see her again.

She'd kissed her fingertip and brought it to my lips. "I'm not letting you go that easily."

I still wanted her.

If I'd had the choice at that moment never to see her again or to marry her, I would have married her—no questions asked—just that sure I'd been right about her. Sure she was the woman of my dreams.

"I'll be raising my baby with another woman," Claudia said.

"What about me?" I argued.

"I never really loved you like that, but I know you've fantasized about this for some time."

"You're crazy!" I hollered.

I had been obsessed with her. Now in an instant, I knew I'd been wrong about her. She wasn't the woman of my dreams. The idea of her was what fascinated me. Not the Claudia in the flesh.

The *idea*. A more-than-incredible phenomenon.

The real me came out the following week. I was ready to be an adult for once in my life, wasn't ready to have some responsibility. I would have someone to love, my own kid. And I would face the brutal consequences and heart-wrenching fears. I would need to grow up, fast.

My moment of clarity came when Claudia and I met for coffee in town a week later. She used the longest sentences she ever had until she finally got to the point.

"I can't have kids, Georgie."

Gulp.

"My tubes are tied," Claudia said, "I just wanted you to be honest with me. I like you. I fucking love you. I do, Georgie. I don't want to be such a crazy girl anymore. I just want simplicity."

I knew she was lying. There was no way she loved me.

I never knew what a wake-up call was until that afternoon over a particularly strong cappuccino. The blend was just as sweet, seductive, addictive, stale, pungent, and dark as the person I used to be and the person Claudia Nesbitt would always be.

All that time, I was trying to be safe, and doubling up meant security to me. I moved out of town a few months later and never saw Claudia Nesbitt again. She fucked me, and she fucked with my head. Still, I loved her. In my own twisted way. She wouldn't really ever change.

Who was I kidding? The affair I'd had with Claudia has caused unbearable confusion in me, especially looking back on the relationship as it might have happened. Claudia's taken everything of worthwhile substance out of my past thirty years— my lifetime—as I blame her for having scrambled up my entire sense of self.

I'm in a stupid metamorphosis, shit . . . and by the time the demons overcome us, you'll know for sure that we, that Georgie's, disintegrated more than you might have imagined. By the end, when wondering, and wondering, something terrifying and blissful, a daydream will have been fulfilled—a reward to no one—or maybe to a handful of a few lucky people.

. . .To the fans of Georgie Gust: We love you. You're our hero to love.

3. MR. CLEAN

It's always late September, the beginning of fall, when the air is crisp, the leaves are always changing, and the light is always fading. It's never winter, it's never spring, never summer. Always fall, always September 1987, when the builders are renovating our house. I can't get away from the noise and the smells. My mother says it's too cold to go outside, and all day long there is the whine of the drills and the smell of freshly sawn wood assaulting my senses.

I'm eleven that year, living in suburban New York, three houses down from New Jersey. My mother reminds me daily: We are not from New Jersey. My mother is very clear about this. She says only niggers, spics, and white trash live in New Jersey, and that's most definitely not where we're from.

I don't care where I'm from. All I want is to go outside, where the leaves on the maple and sycamore trees are changing. I want to go outside, where the world's in color: red and gold, the sky a brilliant, vivid blue, a Georgia O'Keefe kind of blue. I want to go outside, ride my bike, but my mother says it's too cold out. She's lying. I can see it in her face, the way her eyes shift to the left, when she tells me, her lips pursed tight, "No, Benjy, it's too cold. You'll catch your death."

How prophetic. I've been trying to catch 'my death' ever since.

My mother doesn't want me to go outside because my father's now in the process of divorcing her, and she can't take being alone.

Our family structure is typical of an unhealthy one. I've taken on the non-rigid roles of father and son, or rather husband and son. My mother never says she's lonely—not to me—but she tells her friends, especially Rita, the one with the short hair and long, painted nails who comes over Tuesday and Thursday afternoons to play canasta and drink gin and tonic: "I can't take it, Rita. I just can't take it being alone like this. I can't take this."

"Now, now," Rita says and pats my mother's hand until my mother starts crying that she's not going to make it and what is she going to do and Rita finishes off her third gin and tonic.

And that's why I can't go outside. Because it's not Tuesday or Thursday and because Rita's not there to keep my mother company, and my sister, who is only three, is too little.

So instead of going out, riding my bike like I want, I kneel on the nubby white couch, resting my chin against the back cushion and staring out the window, listening to Mike Nova, the contractor, who's sitting at the piano in our living room—my mother's living room, white and stark and modern, blindingly white—droning on, trying to woo my mother into getting more for her buck, trying to convince her to expand the renovation, which she does. Nova turns what began as a simple renovation into something more like an entire second home built onto the original home. It will be my mother's final hurrah, her last dip into my father's money well, which my father will try to keep from her. They'll be divorced within the year, and my father will be paying through the nose, but I don't know that then.

All I know is that my father's never around anymore, and I can't handle it. Pops told me early that morning he'd be home that night, but then he's not, and I spend the whole day in my own secret loneliness, a somber weariness alone, staring out the window at the trees and the leaves and a bald albino jogger I've named Mr. Clean. He passes around the corner of our home. Though he looks old and big and strong to me at eleven, he can't be much more than twenty—young—with the grace of a cheetah, a predation never realized. He just runs, every day, no matter the weather, around the whole block, the whole town, with his white T-shirt that never shows any sweat and his white mailman shorts and a cross necklace bobbing to the beats of my head. He never stops. And it doesn't matter if it's Christmas, New Year's, or any other holiday, he runs every day all day long. I'm the only one who ever sees him, and sometimes now I wonder if he was a hallucination, running around and around my brain. I don't know.

But late in the day, that day in September of 1987, I thought of him as a porcelain stallion of sorts, perhaps terminally ill, with nothing more meaningful to do than run his day, his life away. Even at night, I'd watch him from my bedroom window—he'd be there eventually. Here he comes, Mr. Clean, Mr. Clean.

4. STARSTRUCK

There was a time when Moms and I sort of had our distance, at least temporarily. I was attending Suffern Jr. High School in New York's Rockland County by bus—and don't get me wrong, I fucking loved taking the bus . . . I was usually the last stop coming home, and the driver, when it was Ole Charlie, would pull over just around the corner from our house and swing open the school bus door. I'd get out with him, and we'd smell the blooming lilac bush on the property owned by the famous, or rather, infamous Old Man Harting. Harting was somewhat of a Boo Radley character; he was hermit of sorts, hardly here, hardly there at home, maybe he was just sitting by the TV. This runaway Nazi who "fled the Nuremberg hearings," or something—we kids didn't fully comprehend why he was famous, or if he even was famous, in the history books, somewhere, maybe . . . we didn't exactly understand. Harting, legend told, had once "escaped" to South America—we thought, 'what a vacation'—but he ended up in Suffern, New York, of all places. All of us kids in the neighborhood were all under the impression that Harting had hanged a couple of German Shepherds, maybe more, in his barn. We believed that because our parents had told us, they'd said he was 'mysterious,' and it was this *mystery* that intrigued us so, besides the mystery of why he was so 'famous,' as if we might have seen him on TV or something, but we hadn't had a good clue about whose face to look for. I wasn't allowed on or near his property, but thanks to Ole Charlie, the substitute bus driver, we'd at least get to smell Old Man Harting's flower bush and contemplate his identity. And, by the way, a group of us pre-teens, some from the old tree-house gang, and even my little sister, did end up paying Harting an adventurous surprise visit one day; Harting was sitting alone on his porch. That is another story, altogether, although, in fact, we did hear the ghost dogs barking for help in his ratty barn next to the main house, and we did learn a little later in school that Harting, Nazi or not, was famous for nothing.

My living situation at home, with my family and with school, was unclear to me. Difficult as the memory is now, it seems that a blip in time had occurred during the first few months of my parents' divorce proceedings: by the middle of the eighth grade, I was waking up at 4:30 in the morning in Manhattan and being driven by chauffeured limousine to the usual public school north of the city near Mom's—a two-hour ordeal. Even though I'd choose to sit up front with the driver, I just wasn't comfortable in the back, limousine or not. The kids at school really began to hate me.

And one afternoon, I came home (to the Upper East Side penthouse), and walked in on my father and the any-minute walk-in "surprise"—a famous Emmy-Award-nominated Los Angeles "celebrity" who was "a new friend" of my father.

This . . . is Gladice.

At the time, she stood before me in her teal blouse and white tennis skirt, with her poofed dark hair and an immaculate silver strand dangling with her bangs and her chewed-up dwarfed fingernails; she stood about five and a half feet tall and exhibited the most perfect manners and etiquette.

It was around this time in my life that I found myself burdened with a real nervous demeanor and internal blood flow when I was around famous people. I maintained one of those creepy sneaking-up-on-me half-erect boners, especially if the celebrity was female, and my lips would quiver; I couldn't speak clearly and would lose a lot of my English, even though English was my first and only spoken language. I'd sort of stutter and get stuck when these famous people would enter my senses in reality.

I came out of the bedroom, having just turned off the static on the television; Pops didn't get the Playboy channel, so I all I had to work with was the X-rated images jumbled within the static, I'd find part of a tit here and butt cheek there—the volume turned down to an absolute minimum. Not exactly a big upgrade from the *National Geographic* mags filed in piles in the basement of Mom's place. Unfortunately, I had had enough of the TV, unrelieved, for I heard company coming through the front door. No doorbell, just an unfamiliar "I'm home, honey" in a strange woman's voice, I was already a little starstruck, even though I wasn't in her presence yet, so I walked out in my own shy junior high schoolboy way, a big ha-ha-I'm-in-puberty smile, with my big horn-dorky overbite, my submissive, Eat-Me-Alive-If-You-Must abused child slouch, and a few nervous tics here and there.

My dad was gleaming. "Benjamin," he beamed, "this is Gladice. . ."

"Hi Ben," the celebrity Gladice bubbled, with an air of passive-aggression.

My boner softened a bit—shit—and I replied, "Hi."

The moment turned extremely awkward as my father started carrying her numerous black-leather suitcases into his bedroom. As Pops was coming in and out of the living room with the luggage from Nashville, he said, "Ben, *this is Gladice*, come on, Ben, Gladice is the famous person I was telling you about."

"When?"

"What do you mean when? Just a few minutes ago."

I peeked over at the statuesque Gladice, but I couldn't recognize her. I was becoming physically uncomfortable; she just seemed to stand there, as if waiting for me to talk to her. How does one just 'talk' to a real celebrity?

She looked at me through her oversized sunglasses with her head kind of tilted, as if she wanted me to ask her about her job or to tell her that I recognized her. But I still didn't. She was completely unfamiliar to me.

"So," I said to Gladice, or rather I asked as if I didn't know, "you're famous?"

And she explained, "Well, not here in New York, but in LA, in some other cities, I am, I'm sure famous. I even sign autographs if someone asks me politely."

Not one for words, this Gladice.

With increasing anxiety, I began to tell Gladice about my little Pac-Man scrapbook, which I'd began filling up with autographs of famous people I'd met back in the sixth grade. I attached different memorabilia (I always pronounced "memorabilia" without the slightest of stutters, by the way, like a real collector) from all the "fame"-oriented events from my father's business contacts—movie studios like Lorimar Pictures, you know, I had shit like pins and pens and stuff from television's *Dallas* as well as a New York Giants bumper sticker with some random autographs on the next page, even some scribbles from my famous baseball player second cousin and a sig from some soap star celeb-chick who lived in the same apartment as one of my geeky first cousins, Alvin, who lived on the Upper West Side near the ABC studios. I reminisced while Gladice paid great attention to my pathetic speech: "I waited outside that particular apartment for her to come home . . . just so she'd write me her name, for possibly . . ." and I kept to myself that I had thought she might've been waiting for me all along, in my very private, very personal kid fantasy with the star-next-door. Gladice seemed like the epitome of all the famous people in the whole universe. This one, I figured, I'd better ask this Gladice for that goddamn fucking well-deserved and needed autograph right away, before she disappeared again into the world of fame and bright lights and resumed having relationships with real men, not twerpy little boner-bitten kids like me. Anyway, Gladice was only slightly impressed, and I told her that my scrapbook was at my mother's house in the suburbs. But . . .

"Can I have your autograph?" I asked, as politely as a kid like me could ask without fucking begging—I was already imagining how it might look in print if I were to be its proud owner any second from now. *Might even be worth money,* I thought, aroused by the thought, just plain fucking aroused down there in puberty-land.

She bent lower to meet my gaze and smiled, her eyes widening slightly. Those big "poofy" eyes—and then she suggested a polite "Please?" God, is that all I had to say? Would I have to put hot fucking fudge and a big, big, big cherry on top? Would I have to eat the whole sundae for her, for Gladice . . .

I was more nervous that I'd ever be in my entire life. I was nearly convulsing, boner here, boner gone.

"May I *please* have your autograph?"

"Name?"

(Oh God, what was her name again? What is her freaking name . . . 'This is . . .?')

"May I please have your autograph, Miss Crapella?"

"Yes, you may, Ben."

And I watched her as she pulled a fancy pen from her oversized, totally '80s teal handbag and a business card from her engraved business card holder. She signed the same business card that I would immediately discard as soon as I could find a garbage can that didn't belong to Pops or Gladice. God-for-bid they start hunting for it later or find it somewhere where it shouldn't have been, like unflushed in the toilet . . . like anywhere but within my heart, you know. Obsessing over the signed card—it appeared to be a very personal rendition of a heart, written in calligraphy, totally from the heart, with a simple "Gladice," as in, 'Love, Gladice,' oh my, in complete cursive, script-printed light blue ink slightly off to the side of the heart, with a little overlap.

And I could never forget to say, "Thank you," to Gladice, as gratitude was the single most important lesson I was to ever learn from this hot new couple—from these prize-winners, Pops and Gladice-fuck.

That night, Pops and Gladice slept together as I slept in one of the guest beds. "Good night, Gladice," I'd whisper softly to myself that night. I might have just had the most influential introduction of my life to date, that night. "Bless my life, Lord . . . Let me dream of peace tonight, for she's just in the other room, with my own father . . ." My father would never react the same way to me as he did to Gladice; that's been true ever since, is true even to this day. I was shattered yet again, in some other twisted way. I became the invisible son with a physical presence. I became the third wheel.

And I still had a shitty mother that I would have to go home to within a few days, as I'd later discovered that Gladice and Pops had basically been married since the day I received my autograph from hell.

Twenty years later . . .

"Ring . . ."

"Hello?"

"This is Gladice . . ." This is all I know about her. This is my beautiful stepmother. This is how she answers the phone. This is me, Ben, being sarcastic and bantering about her, about Gladice. The Tourette's rumbles up inside me as I begin to bark. "Rrrr . . . ruff," I snarl incompletely, "Ruff—Gladice, grrrr—this is Gladice, ruff."

She prefers to call me "Ben"; she writes Ben—B-e-n. Not Benjamin, even though I might feel like, ya know, "getting her back"—well, not getting her *back*, I never wanted her in the first place—but by getting her back by blaspheming the syntax of her name by writing her in as Glad Ice or even as one-word: gladicecrapella, thereby causing her to be a noun, not a Proper Noun. My stomach might settle a little bit better, better than if I hadn't wanted her in the first place, since I've come to realize that I want her now more than ever. I'd like to use the word "sacrilegious," but I can't. I dig inside, and I realize that I've always wanted her, even more than I've ever wanted Claudia Nesbitt, my dream woman. I need Gladice. I need to get to the details so that you know what I mean.

#

This is Gladice . . . She was a cute and sweet little girl, Li'l Gladice, the five-and-a-half-year-old girl . . . who smoked her mother's cigarettes in the Bay Area, California. I don't care. Now she is tall, about five-five, and she has teeth implants, a *six-figure mouth,* she brags—her fucking teeth, which used to be all fucking dwarfed and gumlines, are now beautiful. She loves wearing all black, all the time. The silver streak in her shoulder-length, otherwise dark brown hair has been there most of her life, and all of us know that it is a natural beauty mark—not anything she's dyed herself or anything, she insists, and I believe her. I believe my father, who not only insists that I respect her as his wife but who insists that she loves me and that she has been going out of her way to help me, to love me. What a woman to love!

I jerk off to her and feel shame. Feel what it might be like to fuck my stepmother. To fucking fuck her. I feel fucking shame and guilt and . . . I feel my self.

5. DR. CHRISTINE MEETS BEN

I've never had a client like Ben Schreiber. Or, should I say, Benjamin J. Schreiber, as he prefers to be called. The first time I met him, he showed up late, dressed in Armani jeans, a USC sweatshirt, Hugo Boss loafers (no socks), and an oversized blue stovepipe hat with an orange pom-pom on top.

I reacted negatively, I admit it. Clients who show up late for their first appointment set a bad precedent, and I prepare myself for the worst—that they'll not be cooperative in treatment, that they'll not take their meds, that they'll not discuss their issues. I like punctuality. Rich clients who show up late, who have limo drivers and trust funds and are seeing me only because they have fathers capable of keeping them out of jail—they set my teeth on edge; like it or not, first impressions matter, even in therapy. And the fact that Ben didn't even try for a favorable first impression with me set me up not to like him. Of course, a psychiatrist doesn't necessarily *need* to like her clients, but it doesn't hurt.

His being late was bad enough, but his hopping into my office, first on one foot and then the other, as if he hadn't a care in the world, drove me crazy. It's not often that a client can drive me crazy, but Ben did—especially that first day. Later, after I'd read his file, I felt ashamed and a bit negligent in my care, for Ben has Tourette's, and the hopping is involuntary, as is the sniffing and brow-raising. However, I didn't know that at the time. Ben was a referral from the Pasadena Police Department, which hadn't sent over all the paperwork. That said, I should have seen to it that I had his files from the start, as they'd have made a difference in my perception of him. As it was, I let my bias against the rich and privileged get the better of me, and it showed.

Ben sat across from me with his legs crossed, the stovepipe hat in his lap, and smiled. He'd been telling about holding up the Pasadena City Bank with a cell phone in his pocket, and then he stopped, uncrossed his legs, and leaned forward, elbows on his knees, and stared into my face. He looked earnest and engaged, slightly shy, as he asked, "You don't like me much, do you?"

How do you react to something like that? My first instinct was to lie, to say, "Of course, I like you." Instead, I responded professionally. I smiled and said, "My job is neither to like nor dislike you, Ben. My job is to help you."

He nodded as if he understood. "Probably be easier to do that though," he said, "if you liked me. Don't you think?"

I flushed then, embarrassed. It was as if Ben could read my thoughts, and I can't say I liked it.

He continued. "It's okay if you don't. Like me, I mean. If I were you, I wouldn't like me. Hell, I don't even like me."

By then, I'd managed to get my distance and my professionalism back. I leaned forward and smiled—reassuringly, I thought—and said, "That is precisely what I am going to do, Ben, help you to like yourself."

He gave me a sad, slow smile, looped his hands behind his neck, and said his liking himself was not something he knew how to do, but if I wanted, he'd try.

I said I wanted; he said okay, then left.

6. ROUTINE

He could do it. He knows he could do it. If he just weren't such a goddamn nice guy. It's his problem. His condition. His pathology. He's too goddamn nice for his own good. People take advantage of him.

Like Claudia. Who told him she loved him then started fucking Sara and Sara's husband Greg, sometimes at the same time, and would call Georgie afterward or during and tell him it was his cock she was riding, his dick that was filling her pussy, and that she was sorry, but she just couldn't be with him like that. Not anymore. Not sexually. Not when his conditions, his pathology, were so much worse than her own. Like he was fucking contagious or something.

Diego comes into the bedroom then, doesn't look at Georgie. Diego is polite, pretends he doesn't smell the sweat, the cum on the sheets, doesn't notice Georgie, hand under the covers, holding his cock ready to jerk off. Georgie wonders if Claudia's right, wonders if maybe his own brand of craziness, his own peculiarities (better word, Georgie decides, than pathology, which reminds him of a forensic pathologist, reminds him of *CSI* on CBS and how his own script is still languishing somewhere on the back lot at Paramount) really are any worse than anyone else's. He doesn't feel crazy but then maybe nobody does.

Finally, with Diego's back to him, Georgie swings his legs out of bed, pulls on his boxers.

Claudia Nesbitt. It seems like she was, and is, a real person, like Heidi Berillo. But only Georgie could see that Claudia bruised easily, see the little marks of black and blue on her arms and ankles that confirmed her reality. Georgie collects those details, keeps her real in his mind, remembers the scar on her ankle bone. The left one. And how she told him, in bed, sitting up, her legs spread wide, letting him see all the way up her pussy. Georgie remembers that, too, remembers how it was impossible—fucking impossible—to take his eyes off her pussy, the pubic hair clipped. The folds, the recesses. The smell. He loved that smell, loved burying his nose in her pussy, in her cunt, breathing in her smell. No douche. No spray. Just pure Claudia.

Or not so pure. Georgie doesn't remember Claudia pure. Or clean. He remembers the smell of her, how horny, how wet she'd get before her period, how milky, how sticky she'd be, how always before her period, her pubes would tangle, clump together, and she'd always want him to go down on her. Clean her off, she'd say, and Georgie would. But only before her period. Never after. Never during. Just before. She drove him crazy.

Always sitting with her legs spread, letting Georgie look, knowing he was looking, and then telling him stories. About her scars. About her life. Like her ankle. She lifted her leg high above her head, showing Georgie her pussy, her asshole, then told him about her father. How abusive he was. What a drunk. How he threw a knife at her—a Buck, her father was a hunter, she said, and needed a Buck knife to skin rabbits. Then she added that if Georgie ever wanted to buy a knife, ever needed a knife, she'd go with him because she knew all about knives. On account of her father, she said. Georgie would have said 'because of her father,' not liking the sloppiness of 'on account,' but he was in love and didn't correct her. Besides the story of her father and the knife he threw and how she needed thirteen stitches—can you believe it—thirteen stitches on that little tiny bone, she said. And, no, Georgie didn't believe it but he was in love, and it seemed rude to say he thought she was lying, that thirteen stitches are what you get for big cuts and not little nicks on the ankle, so he kept his mouth shut and let her lie.

And now he hates her. He fucking hates her.

He stands in his bathroom, brushing his teeth, saying her name, remembering her scar, her legs, her taste. He hates her—hates her—hates her, hopes she dies, hopes he can sometime stop being such a nice guy, a good guy, hopes he gets the balls to kill her, drown her, electrocute her, cut her. Something. Anything.

A knock on the door. It's Diego, checking on him, making sure Georgie's okay. Has he been talking to himself? Maybe. Probably. More of his condition. His Tourette's, his bipolar, his schizoaffective disorder. Georgie collects diagnoses the way some people collect stamps or coins; butterflies, maybe. He has books explaining every condition he's ever had, and now he worries he's talking to himself. That it's part of the schizoaffective disorder. Wonders not if he's going crazy but how crazy he already is.

"Be right out," he tells Diego.

So, yes, the cleaning crew has finally arrived at our house, Georgie's and mine. Note to self: Is Dr. Christine right? Dr. C? After only a couple of sessions? Is Georgie nothing more than my alter ego? Not a legitimate literary character, a legitimate literary device? And when he dies, when I kill him off—because all literary characters get killed off eventually—what happens to me? Do I cease to exist? Do I care? Life, in my humble opinion, is vastly overrated. And much too long. As I was saying—or was it Georgie saying—the cleaning crew has finally arrived. Daydreams are hitting home runs in the head, Claudia isn't paying rent, taking up all this head space. Claudia is most likely hung over, or something, next door, somewhere.

It is officially afternoon.

Georgie wakes up entangled in a web of slack. I wake up right beside him. Claudia starts her day with cranberry juice and a muffin, eating in front of the TV. And Heidi? How does Heidi start her day? Cranberry juice? Tomato? We can only assume. Her blinds are still closed though, so Georgie and I don't have a clue. Breakfast in bed has been cancelled as far as he's concerned, and he's getting angry just thinking about whatever the hell she's doing, if anything at all. Heidi's probably busy with something, with someone. With Claudia's Greg or Sara. Maybe both. Maybe I'm just being a little paranoid. I pray to know my place in this world, I pray for relief, to understand, to be a better man. I think about that kind of stuff all the time, and I'm sure my creator hears my pleas and is probably tired of all my confessions by now. I'm still in the bedroom, where Georgie gets on his knees for a minute. He gives an hour to his shrink. Every day, it's the same thing. He's barely awake.

Claudia was somewhere else last night. She thought about Georgie often but was with some lady friend. That's what I think—hell, I'm the fucking author; that's a matter of fact. Claudia thought about Georgie all night long.

Georgie rises from his knees, sees there's a message waiting for him. Similar ones will follow throughout the next year.

TUES JUNE 21 9:30 AM: *"Hi, Mr. Gust, Ms. Nesbitt, hi . . . I've been hibernating. I did slip out and go dancing one night. But it was only for a few hours. Anyway, I'm just working from the house for a few hours. Then I've got six clients. Anyway, I just want to say hi and thank you very much for giving me some space and some time. Mmm. I wish you were here today. All right, I'll catch up with you soon. Bye."*

Georgie saves the message—he saves everything of Claudia's—and crawls into the kitchen, barely awake, opens the fridge, and grabs a piece of cold, leftover pizza. There's a calendar on the freezer door. Shit, it's still November. He's been playing the same goddamn message from Claudia for seven fucking months. That's sick, that's what that is. Sick and more than a little sad. Why in the hell can't he get over the bitch?

On his feet, Georgie is full of rage, now that the sun shines through the window, breathing existence and life . . . and light. What a little addict he is, getting angry and agitated because of all the clutter around the house.

Claudia had mild OCD, but she could do the dishes and laundry perfectly. She was a great homemaker, but she was rarely present. Georgie usually had someone else clean up for him.

Fucking housekeepers, good ones, honest ones, a whole family of them . . . housekeepers are a blessing to anyone who can afford them.

Here we are, Georgie and me. Our morning routine has always been sloppy.

I look over at Georgie. He starts cursing and bitching to himself, like any other day, before the coffeepot's even started to brew.

He's been desperate these recent months for his morning routine to bring him something new. Like a run-in with his true destiny, or a random messenger of good news.

We look each other in the eyes. It lasts for only a second.

Packing to leave the house is a pathetic collection of moments. It drives Georgie fucking nuts. It drives me over the edge.

The whole pockets thing: the wallet, the keys (office, home, car keys separately), pack of smokes, lighter, loose change, gum, memo pad and pen, business card holder, booger rag, and dip. Everything's always getting misplaced. Georgie stuffs his pockets and car cup holders in a reckless hurry.

All the drawers in the house become cluttered with so many petty necessities. Yet they continue to get lost with the rest of things.

Georgie tends to overpack as well. He tries not to leave the house often, for that matter. He hates to pack, and he's sick of forgetting things. He feels guilty about this. It's another problem needing blame, like any other problem.

He used to blame his parents. I used to blame mine. Now everything's our own fault.

Georgie was born the reason and the solution. I was born neither. It's taken us years to realize this.

"What a good day!" Georgie declares aloud. "Fucking *fantastic* day!" He stretches his arms out. Big smile, as, for the moment, he's got a positive outlook on the day. But his external thoughts are always running, though they might hide for a second at a time. That's it, a second. They begin to premeditate in his head. Then, they take the lead, unbearable from the very instant they take full charge:

#1. "I emotionally break down and cry when I'm getting head. It's pathetic, but it feels so real."

#2. "I am myself. I don't know myself. I'm still confused about this."

#3. "My neighbor gave me attention. She once saw our little affair as perfect. Later, she failed to come through. I miss her—I shouldn't. She's not worth it. I am obsessed. I can't even seem to think my way out of her. Is she thinking of me?"

But even with the racing thoughts this particular morning, Georgie's head is out of sorts anyway. The symptoms of panic and anxiety have him by the ass. He doesn't know how he might have otherwise created the rest of his day, dreading all the possible upcoming chaos and the required trivial personal exchanges with others that were bound to come up.

Finally #4 rolls on through: "Almost forgot. I want to see my neighbor again. I think she's absolutely incredible."

Georgie thinks he's justified, horny but healthy, thinking such thoughts. Thoughts of her. Thoughts of Claudia.[4]

Loving your neighbor like yourself is impossible. "I" get in the way. It's a conscious thing. Georgie's personality is a contradiction.

Maybe it was lust. He told her he loved her. Did Georgie mean it at the time?

Did he love her when she was out dancing?

Was it infatuation? Perversion? Sex addiction? Addiction to chaos? Addiction to self?

"Shut up. Shut up. Shut up. You sound like your Aunt Beatrice."

But Georgie's got lots of questions.

"That's OK, Princess," he hears Claudia saying.

Georgie's spinal fluid rushes up his neck when he says Claudia's full name, aloud or to himself. Her big hands become an image for his third eye to see. Then her toes. Claudia, like she's from the 1950s. She was glamorous. She dyed her frizzy, dark brown hair that pretty shade of red: Thanksgiving Orange, Outrageous Red.

Yet again, no matter what day Georgie awoke, the dread of putting on his prescription goggles and animating his dull world frightened him. Reality usually hits hard, causing discomfort. Then the look over at the blurry alarm clock he'd beat down the day before with the same fist he stuffs snug in his briefs each night, cupping his balls for a warmer night. A certain kind of misery is born.

He stays in bed for the duration of a piece by Beethoven.

Emperor Concerto, Second Movement.

He slaps the snooze. Half hit. Half miss. All gross. Sweaty and ashamed that he can't get up.

Laziness creeps in. Georgie starts hating himself. He starts to laugh. "Snooze, damn it!"

He thought a snooze was a good nine, ten minutes. Georgie actually timed the motherfucker several times. This piece of crap allowed just over nine minutes of extra sleep time.

That day the thing couldn't have given him two.

It's 1:30, and even at this hour, so far into the day, he is hesitant at the thought of opening the shades, hoping it is not all

---

[4] I never think I'm justified. I question everything. Especially Heidi.

dismal and gloomy out there, trying to picture himself. Maybe if he just stays in bed, Diego will open the shades, save Georgie the trouble of discovering the day.

He closes his eyes, falls half asleep, finds himself in a non-smoking room at the local three-star hotel, hotel hopping. He needs to get away again. We always need to get away. Even if it's only in our head. Geographical change is the easiest fix. Georgie opens his eyes, can't figure out where that three-star hotel's gone. He's forgotten he's still at home.

#

The next day, our place now clean, Georgie can't get out of his head, thinking how much he dreads, how much he resents, the effort needed to take another shower, brush his teeth, and maintain himself, again and again. He did that yesterday. He shouldn't have to do it again. Once should be enough; he needs something different. Georgie craves something different. He's desperate for something new. He'd kill for something new. We both would.

This particular morning, the razor burn on Georgie's neck looks like a leper's chafed jock itch. He can't wait the couple of days required for the skin on his neck to heal, but the realization that he won't have to spend the time and effort it takes to shave until then is comforting. After all, the longer he grows his facial hair out, the easier it is to shave.

Georgie still can't find the right shaving method. Currently, he's on a Panasonic electric for the first layer, then a straight edge without lotion for the second part. Back to a smaller electric beard trimmer, level one for his goatee shadow. No lotion. No cream. No soap.

With so much angst, worry, and despair welling up inside him, Georgie is suffocating in life. While suffering from an outer demeanor he's grown to despise, his pathetic and abused gut is continuously being filled with an extra load of explosive anxiety, worse than tickle torture.

He hasn't been taking risks in his life for some time. The rut where he had been trapped felt so safe. He had no view. The sides were high. All Georgie could see was up and out.

Most things and events don't carry much meaning anymore—Georgie values meaning more than anything else.[5]

Georgie doesn't know what the day will bring. His sloppy routine of rituals: smoking, shitting, showering, shaving, fixing his hair, brushing his teeth, flossing, taking his meds, and organizing, using tons of paper creating lists of things to do, to accomplish, to make him feel productive. His father tells him it's important to be productive.

He looks at the bathroom mirror with the sticker in the corner that reads: JUST TRUST ME.

Right. Like Georgie's going to trust any of the shitty-assed people he calls friends.

Georgie's pathetic reflection looks back from the mirror, a huge ego inflating its head, like an untied condom, all blown up until it screwballs up and away. He guesses he looks all right these days. No, he looks good. He just doesn't know what to do about it. He's so glam rock, and he's smart, like he's got Asperger's or some kind of artistic autism. But he's not sick. His doctor knows that. He can't deal with a label like depression or stress. He feels much worse than that.[6]

When he shaves, the razor makes love to Georgie's skin. When he pees, he aims for the silent section on the water's edge. Afterwards, he tends to fart, poop, and pee again while sitting a little too long on the toilet. Georgie melts into the valued time he

---

[5] I tell Christine as we're in session now that Georgie's self-awareness has been diminishing, and she nods noncommittally. I keep pushing her, saying that Georgie has a veil that keeps him hidden, that he never looks people in the eyes, that he has no idea what color his parents' eyes are. Finally, Christine's had enough; she purses her lips, crosses her legs, lets her open-toed, high-heeled, backless sandal slip from her foot, and leans forward. Intent on making eye contact. Intent on making her point known. "Ben," she says, "the sooner you abandon the need for an alter ego, the sooner you'll be able to embrace your own feelings, move on from these unhealthy choices. Do you understand what I'm saying?" Of course I *understand* what she's saying, but that's not what she's asking; she's asking if I *agree* with what she's saying, which I don't, so I change the subject, ask her about her shoes, ask if they're Manolo Blahniks.

[6] Dr. C refuses to give me my own diagnosis. She says, "Ben, it's words. Just words." Like I don't understand that? I'm a fucking writer, for Christ's sake.

takes, thinking on the porcelain tank. His thoughts are trivial. They seem important, but they're nothing he would actually act on. Good behavior. It's just a lot of theory. A CD is usually skipping while Georgie's in the shower. It's in the shower that he becomes his own naked self, comes into his true element. He can't see a thing without his glasses, and he couldn't tell you how many wristwatches he's had to replace (not exchange or return) because of their lack of waterproofing and Georgie's forgetfulness. Waterproof watches are never appealing to the eye.

No washcloth. He washes himself by hand with shampoo, not soap. Shampoo works better because Georgie is covered with hair, like me, but I don't wash with shampoo. I use hand-milled, organic soap from Northern California—Sunset Cedar—from a place called Patti's Organics.[7]

Georgie smiles in the shower because he was born a man, and the shower's the one place where he's rarely sexually charged. He thinks of himself as a filth connoisseur. Women's dirty fingernails, anal fetish, anything nasty . . . her already-smoked cigarettes for the shrine, the smell of gasoline and melted hair follicles . . . filth. Georgie hates dropping the soap. He hates all the bottles in the shower. They confuse him and make him think about how useful all these products really are and are not.

He hates falling in the shower. God, what else? They should have a soap dispenser that mixes in with the water like a car wash. It would be a convenience, it would save time. And save energy.

Drying off, towels are so coarse and unfitting. Georgie gets these water scars in between his toes sometimes.

Every day, all this, everything, Georgie doesn't change. Nothing does.

His feet are a size twelve, and he wears shoes all the time. His feet embarrass him. He has a foot fetish. He wears blue shoes.

----

[7] I wonder about that. About Patti. Wonder if she shaves her pits, her legs, washes her hair in a creek.

His legs are still in shape, but he wears long pants no matter how hot the weather gets. His legs embarrass him, too. Otherwise, he's your generic, overweight pumpkin.

His plump belly sticks out. Maybe it's cute and huggy-bearish to some single sex addicts, but the hell if Georgie thinks so. He's addicted, too. He weighs in around 268. His driver's license says he's 168. The picture doesn't even look like him, but the photo came out pretty nice.

He used to be in shape. Now he just recites affirmations.

His passport picture is pleasing. He enjoys looking at images of himself.[8]

Georgie dresses up and blow-dries his hair then curls it. He's got highlights, a WASPy, honky Afro.

My hair is dark, thick, with a bit of a wave. My mother always said it was my best feature. And here I thought that was my personality.

Georgie should have picked out his clothes the night before. All his shirts and pants are at the cleaners, and he doesn't fit into the 32s anymore. He went from a large to an extra-large in the shirts. Georgie recently started to leave them out. He used to tuck everything in and wear a belt. He'll still keep the smaller stuff in the closet. They don't fit, but some of the garments remind him of the past and have nostalgic meaning for Georgie. An hour later, he's dressed.

Breakfast is a chore. He washes the dishes by hand to get his mind off all the stress, feeling a little like things are in slow motion. This activity reminds him of strolling down the aisles in the supermarket at midnight and how hypnotizing it is, the trippy music and the paradox of choice everywhere. Time exists differently at the grocery store.[9]

---

[8] Dr. C tells me this is revealing—that Georgie likes looking at images of himself—and asks if I like looking at images of myself. I sidestep, ask why she's asking. "Do you think I might be narcissistically wounded?" I ask her. "Is that it?" She says nothing, and I am persistent, ask her on which axis of the DSM-IV she'd place me. She smiles, but not like she's happy, and says, "And on which axis would you place yourself, Ben?" Depends on the day, I tell her, on the weather, on whether I've gotten laid.

[9] I have a theory it's the fluorescent lights—that they interfere with the passage of time. You walk into Von's or Ralph's late at night, twenty-

Georgie's out of OJ, and the milk will cause him to have gas, but it seems to go best with the microwave pancakes. Georgie likes his food a little cold, and he dislikes cooking. He presses the "cancel/stop" button twice on the microwave when it's down to two seconds. It's not like he's in any rush.

His keys are in place. He locks the door without checking. Georgie's sick and tired of lock-checking and forgetting important things after he's already left. Georgie, I think, could very well be a loser, but what's that say about me? That I'd create a loser of a literary character, a whiner, a complainer—an agoraphobic with OCD? I catch Georgie out of the corner of my eye and wonder what I've done, giving him all these . . . issues.

He swears he's not going to check that lock, yet he does even though he's only going out for coffee and coming right back. It's not like he's going to plan out his whole life at the counter sipping his cup of Joe, like some romantic poet at the Café Paris.

He brings along his laptop computer, a pad and pen, and a couple of self-help books with the covers torn off just in case. He rarely uses any of these items in public. Sometimes he'll drive to the convenience store and sit in the parking lot. He watches people. He likes watching.[10]

Georgie lights his first cigarette of the day—a Marlboro Light, he worries about cancer—and puffs away.

Georgie rarely finds himself looking forward to dealing with people at all. But he'll usually end up running into somebody, a halfway point to a need, a person who can be a means to his end—running into people, obstacles on the sidewalks and in the elevator, an imperative check-in with somebody who really shouldn't care, and neither should Georgie.

All this whining and baby shit get him nowhere, but he continues to bitch. After his cigarette comes a cup of coffee, then another smoke. A couple of more smokes after that.

He dreads being in line at the coffee shop yet again, only to feel better somehow. All self-conscious and critical with perfect

---

eight years old, you come out an hour later, barely seventeen. It's just a theory, I tell Dr. C, not evidence of disordered thinking.

[10] "Ah, a voyeur?" Dr. C says. "Now *that's* interesting." (I wonder what she *really* thinks.)

advertisement model types in line before him. They pretend they're holding their noses and standing clear of the stench coming off Georgie's sweater. Reeking fumes of tobacco pollution. And they're all so nice and friendly and trivial and guarded. Now that's a challenge.

And still, he's half-asleep.

Georgie's always half-asleep. No matter what I do. Except, of course, when he's thinking of Claudia. It's the only goddamn thing that makes him feel alive.

Now, Georgie's next in line, again. At the coffee shop. Tabitha's working the counter, but Georgie's not paying much attention to her.

7. TABITHA

Service Worker

The coffee shop girl, the soft porn starlet, the hottie behind the counter with sparkles on her face, glitter and tiny bubbles of fun dancing unwavering from her mouth with every gleeful word she delivers. Her smile radiates bright white, and she's far from tired. Her name is Tabitha. I listen to her. She's all, "Hi! How are you?!" She's all happy and shit. I remember when I used to be happy. It's been a while. Now all I want is a jolt. A strong dose of caffeine for that little edge that's so exhilarating to the senses, especially in the morning. I'm looking for a little more anxiety to get me going.

I haven't gotten laid in a year. But still, I scan this postmodernist's figure, eyeing her and outlining all our possibilities as a sexually active couple, through marriage, through the whole thing. We'd work out beautifully together, a happy couple, in love.

Tabitha's about eighteen and undergoing her "I'm only young once" rebellion phase. She wins the award for best teen angst, rebelling when she's got the chance, the chance she can't afford to miss now or find later.

She has magic anarchist/sadist black hair and black fingernail polish that's halfway scraped off. She had a hard time getting permission to have her tongue pierced like she wanted to. It was just as hard for her as it was to lie about the tongue ring's true working function. Tabitha was just as excited to get her first fake ID. Her first hit of Peppermint schnapps.

I know the kind of music she listens to. I hate it. I wonder how long it took her to acquire a taste for those alternative industrial sound puzzles. You never hear them on the radio.

This coffee cashier must have done certain things she didn't expect in order to fit the mold of her strange conception of, you know, the whole concept of BEING YOUNG ONCE or something.

Peer pressure, cat fights, pot, lesbian lovemaking at the junior prom, sniffing glue.

But her behavior with the customers is surprising. The guy in front of me orders some variation of a chai tea drink. She explains to him how they discontinued it, but she doesn't know why. She really seems to know her stuff. I didn't think most employees at fast-turnaround jobs were actually trained like this.

I feel like crap because I've never held a real job. I feel like a real outsider to the current culture. I don't even watch TV anymore.

The guy in front of me decides to order a grande iced mocha instead.

"Good choice!" declares Tabitha, and the gentleman is rung up.

He pays with a twenty-dollar bill.

"Out of twenty? All righty!"

I usually order medium drinks. They're average. Like me.

I don't understand how this girl does it. She's a good worker, doing her job well. She was friendly, indirectly personal, knowledgeable, and efficient.

My turn comes up. I have a plan to tell her something like, "I like your clothes. I like black." Something nice.

She looks me right in the eyes. I realize something, to my sudden shock. She's completely out of my league. My jaw drops. This chick is sexy, really sexy.

As agonizing as it is, my quick little fantasy of her, of us, in my head, heart, and other half lasts half a second until we're walking down the red wedding carpet with rose petals and rice, married, with kids, living in our small villa on the Côte d'Azur, making weekend trips to Paris and London. Right on through to our only natural divorce.

"How are you?" her voice interrupts.

I lie. I lie my ass off. I'm too anxious to speak the truth. I panic. "My wife walked out on me today. I wake up. She's gone, took everything. I haven't a clue about the kids. Please. I need a super-sized vanilla latte . . . *please.*"

I leave a huge tip in the tip jar because I don't need the change. I need cover.

"How are you?" I ask.

All she asks me for is my name. "Georgie."

I want to tell her I'm not lying. I wish I could say, "Nice to meet you," but she starts to look nervous. I need to watch more television, make a priority out of learning proper human interaction.

By the sugar and milk stand, I drop my cup of joe, its contents, all that caffeine, all that tar soup, spilling over the edge of the counter I knock it upon. I turn fire-engine red, red like the Play-Do. It was my mad little attempt to pour out some excess coffee so more milk and more sugar could be added. It runs sour.

Coffee always comes too hot. It's hard to pound it down like a soda or beer without altering its temperature. I pick up a used *New York Times*, there in Los Angeles. I sit outside taking hits off one of the last two smokes left in the pack, hoping no one will ask to bum off my lucky smoke.

But somebody does, some hardcore crackhead lady who looks a little like me, like I used to look, all cracked out, way back when. She wears blue Puma kicks, a red sweater, and a cross around her neck.

I read the real estate ads and dream a little. I no longer need that jolt from the java.

Sweet as Tabitha was, strong as my man muscle is, black as my eye would be the next time that sexy woman inside might speak to me about some silly coffee, as plain and as boring as my dreams are, I should have nothing else to want. When there's no conflict, everything's okay. But everything's not okay. Not now. Others tell me I haven't seen anything yet. So I wait with some patience. I start talking to myself in the parking lot, bugging out. "Tricks are for kids," and other mutterings of nonsense.

I was in love with Tabitha, if that was even her name. They don't wear nametags at coffee shops. I need a wife. I deserve love. That's the honest truth. There's no need to get all poetic about it.

8. PREGNANT WITH THE IDEA OF GEORGIE GUST

I ask myself again and again when the idea of Georgie Gust had initially been planted in my womb as a seed of sacrifice, whether my own sacrifice was something that had happened sometime back in sixth grade, in Mrs. Petite's classroom, or whether it was when I gave up my virginity. Was I impregnated with the idea of Georgie at all? During some point while I was fucking Kathy Friedlander in our little childhood tree house? I'd say he was born by the time I encountered Heidi, but had I even been Georgie's father in the first place, or his mother . . . and his mother? Could Mr. Clean have been his father? Was he even real? Is he now? I imagined Georgie a hell of a lot more vividly once I'd begun writing about him, although once I started to write, another unproductive season of writer's block started to weigh me down and I couldn't handle everyday stress too well and I gave Georgie the qualities I didn't like in myself. So is it when I'm in love that I start or stop writing? Is writing the end-all cure to my mental maladies? Either way, Claudia has been the woman I want, and the way I'd always imagined Georgie's shooting through his mother's birth canal had nothing to do with me, which is probably the reason why he is such a mystery to me, as much of one as I am to myself. I mean I can't even hold a thought together. I'm terrible at transitions. Try this:

Georgie's parents were about to be busted in a motel for cocaine. The room was filled with smoke. The fire alarm was blaring. The lovemaking was equally passionate. The phone was ringing off the hook.

Finally, his young, soon-to-be mother snapped in a sexual frenzy. Threatening, sadistically, to the father-to-be: "Get me pregnant," she commanded. "Just do it!" And she slid off his rubber.

Papa's socks were still on. He wore a thick '70s moustache, true porno style.

The paid-for couple was on fire, heated in ecstasy, fucked up on a drug-induced high.

Suddenly, Pops made that ever-so-agonizing announcement, "I'm going to cum. I'm going to cum!" Then he spat out, "Cumming!"

Just as he let half of Georgie through the gates to his mother's safe haven, through the door of the motel room came a raid by a half-dozen cops and the DEA. Talk about being in the wrong place at the wrong time and being scarred for life.

Details of the constricted, stressed muscle-spermie . . .

The newborn child showed early signs of extreme fear and began acting out nervous habits before he was two years old. As a youngster, he was withdrawn and considered an outcast. He didn't have much self-esteem. He, too, later got into drugs. His life often seemed hopeless and burdensome. This scared little kid was often sad, caring toward others, thoughtful of others. By his early twenties, he grew a slightly offbeat sense of humor. This kid's still alive today.

He was diagnosed with Tourette's syndrome with concomitant paranoid features, bipolar depression, schizoaffective disorder, and other bullshit by the time he got out of school. He obsesses over his afflictions and uses them to excuse his strange behavior.

One day this kid had his first experience of feeling—feeling something besides irritation, anger, or depression. It was a feeling resembling that of despair.

Georgie was entering a new stage in his life. It seemed to approach him in spurts. Then the big finale came. It took him over completely, about a year later.

Flash forward a little while—the big one.

He sat there crying, crying his heart out. There was nothing "baby" about it. His heart was bleeding. The ink in his pen painted the page with profound change. He let go and allowed his heart and soul to drain until they were both empty.

For a full hour, he lived a metamorphosis, an ugly old life blending into something beautiful and extraordinary. He couldn't put words to anything he thought. His legs and hands trembled. Everything old and ugly turned into a positive memory. The past was recreating itself while the present still existed. Something remarkable and intangible had taken over all of his senses.

This kind of experience, which might have lasted only a moment, instead lasted his whole life until now. Everything poured out at once. It wasn't an epiphany, nobody died. It wasn't anything stretched into some tall-tale exaggeration. It was real. It was genuine. It was beyond what any language could convey.

The man who was crying with such intensity and purpose was by no means a hero. He was someone I knew. He was common.

This was the same man who was once a stupid little kid stuck in the principal's office, silent and lost in thought during the pledge of allegiance. He was fined with a sense of humiliation for not participating with the class.[11]

This was the same rotten, out-of-shape, wannabe writer. He finally completed something in his life. Sounds familiar.

Ladies and gentlemen, assume the position.

This was Georgie. Separate from me. This is who Georgie is.

FADE IN:[12]

Maybe things had started with the birth of the idea.

---

[11] This was also the same drug addict who, years later, held up a non-cash bank just after 9/11. He demanded a million dollars using his cell phone as a weapon. He claimed to be a terrorist since his ZIP code was 91101, since at the time he was living in Pasadena, California. He had ID and avoided jail by touring several mental wards and rehabs. His daddy was sending money his way, he hated his father, yes, even once Georgie left the Gust family back in New York. Georgie lived on trust after trust fund. Trust that he would be able to impress the family once he was out there, making it big, that he could overcome being as possessed by the Devil as he's selfishly believed that his parents were. I blame Georgie, my alter ego, my fucking life and pride. I loved my own family, in contrast to this Georgie. Okay, it's a sensitive subject. Any shrink would agree. But back to Georgie, this was Georgie . . .

[12] Let me lose my mind while you listen, look, and loathe.

9. THE BIRTH OF GEORGIE GUST

I'm not sure if the existence of Georgie, Georgie Gust, was actualized before my senses as a result of my sobering up or as a figment of the world in my head once I had been approached by Heidi Berillo, the real person, the brief encounter.

As I'd been clean for some time, the confusion swarming in my head was exacerbated. To this day, I'm unclear why.

Heidi Berillo bruised easily, and the little marks of black and blue on her arms and ankles confirmed her reality. Having approached me one morning on my way to the convenience store, her presence, her poise, and her imperfections caused a sudden thunderbolt in my heart. Okay, it may not have been only a fucking day, fuck, whatever, it's embarrassing.

Anyway, the thunderstorm would certainly last more than a day, more than a while. Heidi would take on a new name once the idea of her was born. After she left, she was known to Georgie and to yours truly, Benjamin J. Schreiber, as—our private Perplexity—Claudia Nesbitt. It was love at first sight with her, every day—every fucking day.

Stendhal, the famous French author from the mid-1800s, once wrote something like "that ridiculous word ought to be changed, but the thing called love at first sight does exist." And, stone me! It does.

My spine sent down shudders when I thought of her, still— her frizzy, red hair, pale skin . . . her sex and her sensuality. Knowing that we could have had a perfect relationship because we didn't have much of any relationship at all made me just as sick as it caused a stoppage in time.

I can remember Georgie flitting before my eyes like the Shadow People, who used to dance when I was getting high. This was Georgie Gust causing sensations in me, causing me to realize someone I know very well whom others can't see.

His life is much more interesting than mine. But, at the same time, I am this person. Georgie Gust is the feeling I get when I think of his name. The drama and chaos I find inside, I find in him. The clarity of the environment he shows me. Yet the same

Georgie Gust is a part of me. He is me. We are the same, different, but the same. It's a really fucked-up phenomenon.

I'm merely a spy, an observer, into the world of my hallucinations. But Georgie's hallucination of Claudia Nesbitt is that of the very woman I desire more than anything in the world. The only thing left in the world I want. But who am I? What do I truly know about myself?

. . . I'm still stuck, still thinking about myself so I think again about why I want—I want, I want—I want, God, she's just such a flat, boring person, that Claudia. Why should I "want" her? Because I think she's changeable. After all, I can think what I want about her. Perhaps by changing Claudia Nesbitt, her alterations will reflect in Heidi Berillo. She's fucked up and I love her, I think, but my very own Georgie Gust has the key to create my ultimate Perplexity through the creation of his ultimate Perplexity.

Wait, what am I talking about? She's a character in my distorted mind. I'm drawn to her complexity, through my loneliness. I might mix-and-match the traits in her that I want in myself, and the other way around. I might build her up like a CSI composite sketch and get off to the final portrait. You might as well hate me now, if you haven't already. I'm trying to figure everything out. My feelings, beliefs, and opinions are not solid matter—they keep changing. This must be the stuff of life, the stuff of perplexity.[13]

I remind myself about Georgie and how he'll get off, pretty much every night and every morning, especially when he's tired.[14]

---

[13] **per·plex·i·ty**: Intricate, complicated uncertainty, tangled confusion, involved . . . complexity, a condition resulting from something that *perplexes* . . .

[14] Georgie would create full-on erotic fantasies from the images of the various body parts of different women whom he'd meet in my day-to-day living arrangement. He'll come up with the head of one woman, the ass of another, the tits of someone else. Left tit and right tit separately and the nipples separate themselves. The foot of so-and-so, the toes of someone he saw in a magazine that day, and so on. Until he's got a Frankenstein blow-up fuck-me-suck-me doll fully fledged out in his mind. He gets off to this kind of thing. So do I.

Make me smile and decapitate me. Play soccer with my bloody thoughts. Tell me I'm creatively horrifying. Voices of coprolalia cause repeated heart attacks in me. Love me. Hate me. Fuck me. Kill me. It'll only be a matter of time until you do anyway.

Give me a paper cut, right on my eyelid, on the corner of my mouth. I'm so lonely up here. I'm ready to die now, ready to swim into the realm of strange mental disturbances. And now it's starting to pour outside.

I watch in wonder.

10. ON GEORGIE

Georgie's life, oh it's a mess. What does that say about my life? My persona? Are we both flawed? Can we save each other from our own deaths? I think about him now that it's still foggy outside. The morning is approaching through the darkness. No stars, no moon. Just me, sopping wet with no fresh towel. I'm out of the shower, watching a re-run of the morning news. At least it seems that way. Georgie's still asleep, dreaming of the past.

The drugs did a lot to him. He dreads his next uncertain move. He's a party pooper, although Georgie's heart tries to remain quiet. His spirit has strange powers; even his ex, Amanda Binet, he thinks of her. She's got a strong spirit, too, flooding Georgie's thoughts sometimes from so far away. He thinks she's somewhere in France, now engaged to a French lawyer. She lives with him and is happy. He finds his conversations with her in his head lonely. He wishes he could go back and be satisfied with going back to her, with her. He fears what lay ahead in any real world. Georgie knows nothing—well, not nothing. He copes with reality by withdrawing from it. His participation in this class stinks. But this is it. This is life. This is the Big One. It's happening right now.

"So what are your interests? What are mine?"

He'd like to be in the moment and help people. But he's often distracted and overwhelmed. He might be brilliant, but he hasn't got the ego or guts to become a real leader. He'll stay right here in his imaginary world of chaos and imperfect, loose thought structure. Georgie contemplates a masturbation session in this public restroom. He's partially dissatisfied with a little of everything. Before he left his house this morning, Georgie found his keys in the laundry room. He turned the dryer back on, just like before and last week. He still dreads the folding job ahead. He wishes he had maids, a driver, a butler, and servants, he'd treat them well. Wishes for friends he could pay for, his memories of them nearly gone. They were once there. He's caught rambling. I shut him up whenever I want. I tie him up. I handcuff his wrists to his ankles. He tries to lay gas. When Georgie's heart peels away at a little truth, he tries to hide it, layering hesitation and fear in tangled letter combinations, words, and theory. That's when I take over.

This is my life. How might I die?

The gray skies have dulled away, and yesterday's rain's coming to a halt. The dew rubs against Georgie's bare feet, grounding him, burning a fire in his mind. Everyone's watching. He's alone and invisible. He can't feel. He can't exist. He's not needed. He breathes. He thinks. But he is not. Georgie wants to say he doesn't care, but he does. I want to care for him, for me.

He wishes he could record all his thoughts and hallucinations with their imaginary universal reflection, i.e., George's personality, but unfortunately, it's impossible. He wants to matter, more and more, but that's impossible, too, because he's there in the distance, aiming a spotlight down at the stage. The play goes on, and Georgie plays no part. He's the guy on the back burner, in the stage crew. The last one picked, the charity case, the delinquent. I feel like his judge. Is he the rich kid with a big heart? Am I the one with a side dish of rage and anger?

He's often depressed, and his moods swing in kaleidoscopic circles. Sounds familiar. Sounds strange. Sounds like me. The fibers in his mind vibrate, and images are formed. The first image is of me, Ben. Georgie's image comes to mind just after that, and my mind hears the image speaking low and pleading, "Kiss me. Fuck me. Kill me."

I realize Georgie only wants knowledge and control of his self, as I want control of mine. He wants it all without delay. I can wait a little longer. He pounds a shot of espresso as if it were a beer instead. Now he might be able to focus better.[15] Georgie tries to fit in, into my life, and he does, but he suffocates within me. He holds his breath in and blows out all the smoke I can't fit inside my lungs. He can't party anymore, just like I can't. Not even on his birthday, that hideous memory he'll never know as I know it. The entire party Georgie's come to crash, it's finished

---

[15] Christine smiles at his little caffeine addiction; she sees it causing him more lethargy. Caffeine never really works to wake me up fully, either. Christine thinks I'm just lazy. I tell her that Georgie is aware that he's is lazy, that it's justified, in a way. He blames his laziness on the time that shrinks around him. Christine calls this nonsense and rips another piece of nicotine chewing gum from her sheet of twenty-four.

with him. I'm finished with him, just not yet. Only been around thirty years so far.

Age is so relevant in Georgie's life. He's fascinated with age. How old are you? It makes a damn big difference. It's real. So is time. So are we. So are all the ideas, the chaos, the mathematics, the collective conscience, medical malady, a boy's yearning for a relationship with his father,[16] love, loss of a lover,[17] losing out, nostalgia, and conspiracy. The latter I no longer believe in. I know better.

Georgie's had déjà vu for the past half an hour. Is it his meds or another medical malady working its magic? He wants a new malady, a label, and I'm six hours late on my meds. I take them now, doubling up against the rules.

He needs reasons, answers, definitions, solutions, and resolutions. He needs more wants. He's got tunnel vision. He doesn't want to get into a car accident on his way home. The possibility frightens him. It's raining hard.

Georgie fears death, his own death, perhaps even mine, and the death of others, loved ones in particular.

He needs this. He needs a better introduction.[18]

I know that Georgie can't stand listening to his inner self. Why can't I listen to mine? He wonders where the borders of his mind are. I tell him how the map inside is incredibly vast, like my own thought plane. I tell him how complicated I see his. At the moment, Georgie is thinking about saving his ex-girlfriend while she saves him in return. But it's pretty unrealistic, he concludes. I question if it would be worth saving anyone else for the purpose of saving myself.[19]

---

[16] Christine asks who 'this boy' *really* is.

[17] My Heidi or Georgie's Claudia?

[18] "Who is he?" Christine asks. "What is he?" I tell her I think he's the scared little kid at Rye Playland, but I don't know for sure. No, he's the out-of-shape smartass who doesn't enjoy reading or TV, he's the guy who's culturally inept because he chooses to be. But Christine just stares off into space. I lean on my knees and insist, "He dwells on the negatives, the positives float on by." "What? Ben, leave Georgie out of this room. When you come to see me, bring only yourself, okay?" "Let me lose my mind," I demand, and she throws me out. "Go!"

[19] I think about Amanda, I'm brought back. Georgie is brought back,

Let me run away, Georgie.

Yeah, run away and leave Ben behind.

Now I'm a little mad at everyone. I suck in the wafting guilt in the air. I have no reason to crave my own death, but I do now. For no apparent reason I'm bitterly angry. Must be my disorder. Must be my fault for sure.

Have I been completely abandoned by my own self? I take my glasses off so I can't see. I want to crack them apart.

Dr. C wants to know about Heidi, about us.

---

too. I met Amanda Binet in a psych ward, where we happened to be together while busy overseeing our simultaneous suicides. It wasn't until our alter egos took on lives of their own that Amanda grew sick and tired of Georgie's alcoholism and rage. Amanda would prolong any breakup, keeping her hold on me, Ben Schreiber, as I'd stick around to actually feel the abandonment. We were doomed from the start; they were doomed from the start. Amanda and I broke up five years ago, and it's been about five years since Georgie's last encountered her. He still loves her. I got over her. Yes, Christine, we disagreed, I want to say, but I'm in the Town Car on my way back home, fucking Christine, with your open-toed fucking *neck brace*, you want me to tell you anything else you don't want to hear? Hell, I'll just take it out with anger. Neck brace . . . so silly of me, stupid anger; what are you trying to prove with your making me try to explain shit. You'll just disagree and roll your eyes. What's the diagnosis, sweetie, stupidity or stress? Suck you! Dr. C! Okay, I'm done.

11. CHANCE ENCOUNTER: REALITY

I woke up early for once.[20]

By 8:30, I walked the shoreline on my way to the convenience store to purchase a cup of coffee and a pack of smokes.[21]

It was windy. I held onto my bright blue lampshade hat with my hand for about a block, until the local hotel screened the big ocean breeze. The Sea Port Hotel was right on the water.

Some hotel guests were in line before me at the convenience store across the street. They found better deals there on both coffee and cigarettes. Hotel gift shops are for those in a hurry and for those who don't care much for variety or value. I never shop there. Guests shouldn't either.

I got my change and tore open the fresh pack of smokes with a medium coffee in my other hand. Then I fumbled, having dropped fifty cents on the pavement.

"What are the chances of that?" I heard.

I went almost completely blind and deaf since I was in the presence of a naturally beautiful older woman. This usually happened to me, especially if she wore open-toed shoes. I'd lose my senses altogether when she had the slightest imperfection of either character or physique.

---

[20] Last night, I'd ransacked my shit little bedroom, cracked my glasses apart in the midst of my rage, overdosed on Advil, and prepared to die. I didn't really know why. I didn't really even know what I was doing or why I was doing it. I just wanted to die because I'm aware of my unattractive anger, and I can't stand it. You could say I'm not one for happy endings. I'm living in this torrid and tortured unidentified self. Last night, I couldn't even jerk myself off; I couldn't bear to lie anymore. Whatever, I wanted to go commercial, you know, get real rich and real famous, then sell myself out completely. You know, lie in a bed of American Beauty pollen and cat and dog dander. Family and friends say I've got a borderline personality disorder now. They call it BPD for short. Do I hate acronyms . . . I tell them that I hate myself, because I do. You might as well.

[21] My fate would be determined beforehand nonetheless, and I wouldn't be dying anytime soon.

"What are the chances of what?" I answered, my own voice echoing in the darkness of my mind.

"You were just singing 'Hotel California,'" she said. "I heard you."

It must have been playing on the radio while I showered that morning. She was humming the melody. I shut up. I looked down. She crushed something with her heel in the parking lot.

"Aw! I stepped in someone's gum," she moaned.

I pulled out a new smoke. "I think it's a Lifesaver," I told her.

She discovered that I was right and said, "But you were singing the same song as me, weren't you?"

I explained, "I don't know. I don't remember."

Here she was. Here entered Perplexity into my world, my life. I would never forget all the data that my senses were collecting then. Bright lights were reflected off her jewelry, then buried in the nostalgic depths of my imagination and memory.

"Well, don't be embarrassed," she suggested. "That's amazing!"

"Yeah," I said.

A vintage black Ferrari pulled out of the lot with its top down. Heidi gave it no attention. The male driver in his fifties probably suffered from the same premature ejaculation that the car did.

I grunted at the thought.

"Hey, you live down on the corner of the next block. You're always smoking cigarettes out front," she said.

I confessed, "Yeah. Probably. Maybe."

"I waved to you the other day," she recalled, "and you just turned away."

She must have recognized the big blue hat.

"I'm really groggy in the mornings," I admitted.

She smiled. "You're really anti-social."

I corrected her. "Not anti-social. Non-social, maybe."

Her face lit up. She started playing with her hair. "I was just on my way to get my nails done. I've been over at the Sea Port for the past week. God, it's this convention for work. It's so boring."

"What's your name?" I asked.

"Heidi Berillo." Heidi had a nametag on. She must have forgotten. "What's yours?" she asked.

"Ben Schreiber," I said, indicating her nametag with my finger. "I was checking to see if you were a liar."

I put my hand out.

"Firm grip, Mister Schreiber." She laughed.

#

Later that afternoon, we were hitting it off together like we'd known each other for years.

"I can't believe you've never given a girl a pedicure."

"Really?" I replied. I wanted to tell her I was a virgin in making love with feet and toes. Hers were perfect.

Heidi's hotel room was strewn with papers and folders everywhere, and felt-tip pens. She lit a joint, became a little feisty. Her hair was frizzy and red, wild like my imagination, like I imagined hers.

I puffed away on my cigarette. I tried to read what she was thinking through her huge brown eyes. Which eye cried for good things? Which one didn't?

I was in the moment. I became an observer of myself. I wasn't my mind. My mind worked for me. Not the other way around. I was enlightened.

For once, some normal thoughts came in, one after the other. It was easier to focus. I wasn't busy judging, analyzing, and making decisions. I was focused on Heidi.

I thought, *Who is her dealer? Where is this woman from? What does she tell herself about herself?*

Heidi's eyes gave me the impression she was experiencing something profoundly empty, like she was dramatically unfulfilled somehow, with voided hope. Perhaps a little like me. She looked right back at me. We had a perfect moment, a true connection. Unfortunately, it ended abruptly. I used caution not to pry into her life, but I was curious to know more about her. I'm not the best at personal interaction. I'm not sure what's appropriate sometimes.

So she asked a lot about me, but I didn't say much in return. Heidi asked me about all the confusion I spoke of regarding what I wanted out of my time here—big philosophical stuff.

I told her all my needs were already being met, that I'd already lived my life in many respects.

"I've had enough experiences with myself . . . All that crap."

And about my dad, who worked hard and provided my family with wealth—my dad, who meant the world to me.

She called my I've-lived-my-life-already bit "Bullshit," and took a drag off my cigarette.

"Are you happy?" she finally asked.

"I'm not sure if happiness is what I'm really after."

I told her I was trying to actualize myself as "a writer," a concept that is still completely muddy to me. I had idealized this image of myself in my mind over the past ten years, but the image kept changing. In reality, I was writing mostly in my head right then. My friends and family wanted me to write something, to complete something, to achieve something. I didn't think it mattered anymore.

"Why not?" asked Heidi.

"It's like I'm too far away, in time, from when I was actively participating in things and enjoying them while they were happening."

"How old are you, Ben?"

"Thirty."

Heidi was under the veil of drugs, but she wasn't paranoid or all tripped out. Inside was somebody genuine and I could see inside, just barely making her out. There was someone real in there. Funny, that's always good to know.

The alarm clock-radio was tuned to Billy Joel's "An Innocent Man."

Heidi said she had recently figured out her life, at age forty. I didn't believe her, and I told her that.

She said she took things very seriously, and that every encounter happened for a reason.

"Every situation, every consequence . . . everything," she added.

I wondered what my role in her life was at the time. This woman, she knew me so well. I missed that. People usually took little interest in others. At that moment, I felt honored and appreciated. I didn't deserve such a luxury.

Heidi finished her joint and pocketed the roach. She slipped off her open-toed leather shoes. Her light blue polish was scraping off like an adolescent's.

"I need a pedicure, now!" Heidi said, smiling playfully.

Toto's "Africa" aired next on the bedside radio: "Frightened of this thing that I've become."

I painted her toes New Blue and left.

I left a note: "Thank you. Ben." I watched her sleep for a half-hour then added my home number below in my usual kiddie-print handwriting and walked out, not really knowing what else to do.

Heidi had a lecture to attend later on as it was.

"Hurry, boy, she's waiting there for you."

Ring.

Click.

"Hey, Ben, I was just thinking of you."

It's all about me now, isn't it? I can't help it.[22]

I took a carefree stroll on the beach, remembering the best parts of growing up. They flooded my mind with nostalgia. I tried to remain in the present.

The moonshine lit up the sand and the whitecaps that were breaking twenty feet out. The tide was low. The rollers were a little choppy, but their sounds were still soothing. I remembered how rich and full my life had been before. I wondered what went wrong. I walked along the water's edge to find some inner peace.

I enjoyed wandering around, engaging in very little activity, comfortable in my imagination, comfortable nowhere. I thought, *Has one year of your life ever been made miserable by love?*

I wondered if my one year of misery was approaching. It was nighttime. I started to dream.

Heidi and I were lost in our thoughts. We took in all that was around us. We were walking the neighborhood sidewalks, holding hands, until coming up to the beach, where the whitecaps intensified in front of us. Huge seagulls flew in with their broad wingspans for their final feasting of the day.

---

[22] You hear that, Dr. C? I can't help it. I can't.

The next morning, the beach was empty. The sky was gray, flat and still, surreal. The gulls flew low in flocks. The long Pacific rollers washed in and out.

We were visiting the past. Oh my, the colorful beauty was so intense; I couldn't stand it.

I was on the phone with Heidi.[23]

"I was downstairs at one of the lectures. It was sooo boring," Heidi was telling me.[24]

"Boring, huh?" I said to Heidi.

"But I got several compliments on my new pedicure," she said.

"Thank God," I said, letting out a sigh of relief.

#

The hotel room had been vacated. I could see it. In the bathroom, there was a wet towel out on the floor, crumpled up from wet feet, wet, womanly footprints. Empty single-serving soap bottles made up for the mess on the corner shelf. A Mexican housekeeper readied the room for its next guests.

I played the message player back again.

"So I thought you might like to know what a great job you did, and on such short notice. Just in time for the only panel discussion I really came here for in the first place."

Her telephone sat on the unmade bed with a box of tissues beside it. Across the street was a fishing pier. A middle-aged couple walked hand-in-hand to the end. They looked out at the freight barges coming into port.

There was a snack and bait stand nearby, but it was still closed at that hour.

A pay phone dangled off its hook.

There was some litter around. Not much though.

"I'm meeting some cool people here, but a lot of them are really bored. This whole convention is really boring."

---

[23] Georgie was still sleeping, as usual, in bed, dreaming of Claudia. In between scenes, he was otherwise having the same pathetic nightmares he found delight in telling others about. His daydreams fizzled out and away, and I've turned into him completely.

[24] I wondered what Claudia was telling Georgie. Was he believing her?

The night before, Heidi and I shared a cherry Slush Puppie on the pier. She popped a few Tylenols (I declined, awe-struck by the sea gulls and shooting stars), as her head was still throbbing slightly from the ennui lingering over her past week at the psych conference.

Only a few fishermen were out with their gear by the morning. It was still pretty early. An Asian man pulled up a small fish. The thing must have been contaminated—the water down below was brown. But his boy grabbed the bucket anyway. It was a keeper.

"So some of my friends and I wanted to hang out by the bar and talk medicine, but I was hoping we could finish our conversation from last night. I really enjoyed walking the town with you."

After the Slushie, we stopped by my place and shared a Winston. I invited her in, but she declined. We took a drive down the coast under the moon instead.

My house was hollow.[25] There was nobody up yet. The whole neighborhood was still asleep. A white van drove past. A newspaper was tossed on the manicured lawn out front.

" . . . at least before I leave tomorrow. Oh, and the weather's so much nicer out here . . ."

Sunlight bled horizontally through the closed blinds in my bedroom, I was sound asleep.[26]

"I was thinking about how brilliant you are," Heidi was telling me on the answering machine. *"And, jeez, you have so much talent. People look at you, and they see big things."*

Expect big things. That's what she meant. Big things, little things. It doesn't matter. It's a stress I can't handle—people expecting things. Anything. Not from me. I live in my head. Alone. I buy porno, coffee, smokes from the snack and bait shop next door, come home. Jerk off. Alone. I'm okay with that.[27]

---

[25] Georgie and I were still one.

[26] Georgie was still sound asleep as well. His eyes were shut tight. He snored like a cow. Claudia continued to soothe Georgie with her voice on the answering machine, and Heidi continued—no, Heidi didn't continue to soothe me. I didn't want her voice on the answering machine, I wanted her. In the flesh. I needed her. I'm not as easily placated as Georgie.

[27] It's Georgie who wants more, Georgie who falls blissfully back to

The clock on Georgie's nightstand read 10:30.

I woke in the morning, glanced at Georgie, didn't wake him, and crawled out of bed. The sky had cleared up a bit over the beach. It was packed with kite fliers. A dozen kites glided over the local coast, full of color and wonder.

The hotel room next door was clean, ready for new guests.

Downstairs, a conference was letting out. The checkout line was out the door. Most of the guests wore nametags on their blazers. The bellboys were busier than hell. They never seemed to get tipped right by the people they would only see once anyway.

There were dozens of fishermen on the pier, more men than fish.

"What would you do if you knew you couldn't fail? What would you do? I love that question . . ."

I walked the beach, having no clue how to respond.

Most of the neighborhood seemed to be outdoors. Most people wore light jackets or hooded sweatshirts. They walked their dogs. They walked their young children. Alley cats ran loose on the sidewalks, and underneath the cars parked on the one-way streets. A few cars passed at ten miles per hour. Pest control pick-up trucks were parked outside one house per block, it seemed.

There was hardly any crime, violence, or vandalism in that part of the city. Maybe some drugs and whatever else went on inside people's private residences, the stuff we'll never know about.

"Grab hold of just one project and get in there with your teeth and see what happens, even if you don't have to," she said. *"Why not? If somebody wants a story about you and you're the only one who knows it well enough, go for it! You'd do the world a favor. Hell, do it for me! I'd love to hear about all that 'crap' as you call it . . ."*

A small gate led to my front door. It was a charming little pad, perfect for a loner like me.

"So what if your dad is some big well-to-do whatever? This is your chance to shine. Just go for it!"

---

sleep listening to Claudia's voice on the answering machine.

88

It's nice having some woman cheering you on. It's the closest thing I know to true love.

Heidi mentioned she had found the perfect little gift in the hotel and she wanted me to call her later.

The orange sun set in between two buildings downtown. I was sprawled out on the beach. It seemed earlier than usual.

Why did I just leave like that? I thought. *What about going back?*

I couldn't change my mind. Reality was hitting me hard. I was scared to go after her like a real man.

Time stopped for just a few exquisite seconds, maybe five or six, until I couldn't bear it any longer. I was self-aware in my newly discovered growth spurt. I was happy.

I started to cry, just out of feeling. Just because I could, just until I needed to stop.

I started to appreciate meeting Heidi, really appreciating her. Maybe I was working through the obsession.[28]

From the beach, I headed back home. I was already beginning to have conversations with Heidi in my head without her being there or being able to answer me.

How lucky she was! Alas! Was this love?

Beep.

"Hey, Ben, I was just thinking of you. I was downstairs at one of the lectures."

Beep.

"Hey, Ben, ugh . . . I'm just calling. I'm sorry. It's this stupid conference. I'm not going to go to this class I have in ten minutes. I'm getting so sick of the same thing over and over again. I'm just in my room taking a bath. Anyway, I'm sorry to bother you. Thanks for letting me vent."

Were we two shattered souls who would end up trying to save each other in a doomed relationship?

The door was swung shut from inside the house. I never got calls. And when I did, I missed them.

"Hello?" I answered.

"Ben?"

---

[28] I thought about Dr. C—Would she be proud of me? Would she congratulate me on my growth? Would she even give a shit?

"You must look so beautiful in that bathtub," I said.

"That was one of the nicest things a guy has ever said to me."

Already back at her place, her lovely feet awaited my attention. She didn't refuse when I administered an oral massage on them while she was still in the bath.

"Right on the arches, Ben."

I loved every minute of it. Her feet quivered with orgasmic delight. Her toes stretched awkwardly.

"I'm . . . sick-dizzy," she moaned, "and you're incredible."

Oh, the gibberish one speaks while in their sexual element, using words that don't mean anything.

"Sick-dizzy," she giggled more intensely.

Heidi had this interesting symptom of pre-orgasm, but I could somehow still understand her in some fucked-up way.

Afterwards, Heidi lay quietly asleep on top of the covers wearing men's pajamas. I headed back home.

We hadn't made love. She must have thought of me as the friendly type, as do most other women. That was fine. I was used to that.

Heidi was a little nutty, but I liked that.

She was a mess, so innocently a disaster—the little Perplexity in my head.

I returned home at three in the morning. I've always loved the night, when everyone else was asleep and the world was all mine. It was quiet and dark—the perfect time for creativity.

All of a sudden, inspiration came. Things got clearer. My ideas made more sense. I could once again install, with a little passion, some letter combinations onto the screen.

I'll have to begin the story from here, with me, as ridiculous as that sounds. It's been forever since I actually sat down to write again . . .

"I never meant to be such a narcissist. I can't seem to get away from myself."[29]

I wanted somebody like Heidi to love. I still didn't know what I needed. Maybe just one tiny success, one simple thing, something in this life that would work out in the long run, to

---

[29] Note to self: This seems important. A revelation, perhaps. Tell Dr. C?

complete something, to get over some things. I needed something good to last.

But by the next morning, Heidi had gone back home. I enjoyed myself and left, too, back to the place where I started from.

I enjoyed myself, it was all that mattered. God probably took delight in watching his orchestration of me that day. I'll call it personal growth.

I never heard from Heidi or saw her ever again.

My mind ran wild with quiet confusion. It felt so soothing to the senses. I would wake up tomorrow, thinking about today, the next day about today.

Was I really a perverted sex addict, like perhaps I *thought* I was or was this some kind of love?

12. SLINGBACKS

The first time I met Dr. C I knew I was going to like her. She had on a pair of slingback, fuck-me, open-toed sandals, even though she knew—she had to have known—that I have a foot fetish. Plus, she had on a clingy, low-cut shirt that revealed the top of her breasts, and she kept leaning forward, provocatively, as she told me that she was going to help me learn to like myself.

I told her I didn't think that was possible (or something like that), but if she wanted I would try. She said she did. What else was she going to say—that she *didn't* want me to try? No psychiatrist is ever going to say something like that, and believe me, I know psychiatrists. I've been seeing them on and off (mostly on) since I was twelve years old, the year my mother decided I had ADD, which was the disorder of choice that year, and marched me off to see Dr. Nora Epstein, the preeminent child psychiatrist in all of New York City, who promptly told my mother that ADD was a manufactured disorder, no one had it. However, as it turned out, what I actually had was Tourette's, which was a thrill for my mother—I was the one and only kid in all of Rockland County, at least in the town of Suffern, at least in Cherry Lane Elementary, to have been actually diagnosed with it, and my mother would parade me out for her friends. "Show them, Benjy, show how you twitch"—but this was not so hot for me.

I'm off topic—a symptom of Tourette's, the inability to stay focused for any length of time—I was reflecting on Dr. C and her desire to help me learn to like myself, which I told her I'd try to do. Emphasis here on 'try,' as there are two problems with Dr. C teaching me how to like myself. First, I can't remember ever liking myself, even before the Tourette's, and second, I think it's fairly clear that Dr. C doesn't like me. Sure, she tried to cover it, but I could read her. Not so much her thoughts as her body language, the curl of her lip when I walked in late. Maybe I'm crazy, maybe I do have Tourette's and borderline personality disorder, which is just the latest in a whole slew of diagnoses, but I still have an IQ over 140, and I know delusion when I see it, and Dr. C was deluding herself thinking she'd ever be able to help me like myself. Still, I'm amiable. I didn't confront her, I just said, "Sure, Dr. C, why not?"

Then I left, went back downstairs to my limo and driver, and asked to be taken home, where I sat in front of the computer, iTunes playing Chubb Rock then Coldplay on a continuous loop, and tried to write. Not surprisingly, I couldn't.

I have writer's block and have had writer's block for the last year and a half.

My guess is that writer's block is the worst place for a writer to be, for most, for most others, other writers. I don't know that for sure. I don't know any other writers, and I don't read anything about them. Don't need to read to be a writer, that's just the way I am. That whole saying: Fuck the Norm . . . But I've got writer's block, I've had it severely for the last year and a half; in fact I haven't written a thing in that time.

While I'm in love, I'll stop writing, for the most part. I know it won't last forever.

"I'm in love." I scoff at the thought.

I think about the present blockage and writer's block as a pleasant break, almost a full-on retirement. I'm spread out lazily on my lopsided bed, and *Heidi, Heidi . . .* Heidi whispers in my ears about my discontent, although I can't make out all that she's saying. I know Georgie's somewhere . . . *Where is he?*

I glance down at my kiddie Billy-Bologne-from-*Pee-Wee's-Playhouse* night light. It's on, and it flickers when my gaze meets the little plug-in plastic lamp. I've saved it all these years. I don't like total darkness; I don't like light, though—I mean I like colors—blue, red, pink . . . I think, sometimes. The see-through shades in my room are drawn shut, the small wooden door won't stop creaking and cracking. I think I'll never wake up in the morning.

And Georgie, *what about* Georgie?

God, I think, *I've been submitting my work for so damn long, I can't stand it, but I'm okay. I don't even know what I'm doing here.*

Georgie tells me to hang in there. "Just go to sleep. In the long run, Ben," he says, "you'll be fine."

Easy for him to say; he's a figment of my imagination, a literary device, a delusion. Maybe even a hallucination. Who knows? They won't tell me who he really is. Dr. C won't—no one will—I'm stuck with this in-between shit, in between diseases, on the borders of some sort of personality disorder, or something.

I had my first encounter, or rather my first experience of Georgie—Georgie Gust—in the sixth grade.

Georgie, Georgie Gust, my alter ego. Mr. Casanova.[30]

---

[30] I unfolded more letters from Claudia to Georgie: seemed like a real lady's man to me. *Georgie, the Definition of intimidation - writing a note to a writer. So I will keep it loose and simple. Find your costume and just show up. —The Girl Next Door*

13. PREDATION AND PARANOIA

I'm going crazy.

Marilyn Skye was the last woman with whom I had a sexual relationship. She wasn't the mistress of my heart. That would have been Amanda. Until Claudia came along.

Claudia was just a desire, just an idea. An idea based on a real woman. On Heidi. This idea of perfection turned to Perplexity.

How did Georgie get her in the first place?

My thoughts come in voices. They speak English. They confuse me. They tell me good things, sometimes.

I feel like crap. My mind is on the brink of an epiphany, or of its ultimate destruction. I'm not sure. I've got to keep everything in order, but it's extremely difficult at the moment.

I'm not asking you to like me. The voice in my head is not the voice in your head. It's not the Word of God or anything. So don't worry.

You might collapse.[31]

Flashback: the soldiers in black uniforms, the clanking of their metal gear as they run through the smoke like Flash Gordons, in my house, in my head.

"You'll be all right."

I thought my lies would save me. I've considered that my past might save me. I'm brought back a little. I'm on the corner bar stool.

I'm alone. I'm a customer, reading the customer script.

Anne's working the noon-to-nine shift. Australian accent, Irish pub.

I listen to Robbie Williams, the Verve, and Moby on repeat on the jukebox.

I pound three double bourbons, the fourth on the house. I pay her a twenty, end with a beer, and stumble home with a heavy head. My house is just next door. I throw up on the floor, then it's off to bed, into my own private world of thought disorder on the Upper West Side of Manhattan.

---

[31] *"Fuck, you're dying. Take another hit and die, asshole."*

I had finished with film school. By that point, I had already received the last letter in the mail from this young woman, the true mistress of my heart. The final breakup letter from Amanda Binet had voided any hope I had left inside. Would there ever be a loving relationship in my life again? Did she love me then if she doesn't love me now? Does love never die? She was The One, just like Melanie and the others.

Amanda and I had met in a psych ward in Harlem, of course it wouldn't last! I was wearing a nightgown, and she smelled like medicine, like dead people, dude.

#

It's noon. I just got out of bed. It was a bad idea to start fucking my neighbor in the first place. How was I supposed to know? That torturing weasel! Get out of my headspace! Now! I still can't seem to get over this woman. There's so much more important stuff, day-to-day stuff, rambling jibber-jabber, nonsense.

Maybe I can learn from this experience . . . I was caught at twelve red lights yesterday on my way to get some coffee. Am I moving too fast?

I'm about to punch myself in the face.[32]

I was a horny little bitch. Now I just jerk off when I need to. Who am I kidding?

I must be getting old, or something. No sexual pride left. I started doing these one-hour jerk-off sessions, trying to help myself get to sleep easier, but I can't cum. I just keep trying and trying. I refuse to give up no matter how long it takes. Maybe I smoke too much. I quit yesterday, how original. So many people die in hospitals. I don't want to. I look at my pack of Winstons. I think better of it.[33]

I'm using Claudia to get all this frustration out of my head.
Name calling . . .[34]

. . . Speaking of which, I've had two cups of coffee this morning and nothing to eat; routine, routine, routine.

---

[32] *"What the hell's gotten into you?"*
[33] *"Fuck it!"*
[34] *"The Princess, the Shark, the Coke Habit."*

I ramble way off the subject; Dr. Christine Morales just listens to me as I run on and on and on.

I've got another doctor's appointment again today, another second opinion. Some of these docs are so fucked up, I swear. One doctor says I've got Tourette's, another says schizophrenia, another . . . blah blah blah. Am I in between diseases? I can live with that; it's cute. But who can I trust, the one on the right or the one on the left? They're all puppets, Muppets, gonzo, sex.

Two cups of coffee, and I'm all over the place. A couple of years back, I would have reacted differently, but I've changed. I skim through my junkie memoirs. I was such a good little kid. I want to swear, but I know some better words. I'm choosing not to use them. I don't want to end up in hell.

In the end, I wondered and wondered . . .

14. BEN'S BANK ROBBERY

Dr. C seems to think that dredging up the past will somehow fix my present. To bring everyone up to date: I'm not in therapy because Dr. C wants to teach me how to like myself. I'm in therapy because I robbed the Pasadena City Bank. No, not really robbed it. More like pretended to rob it. More like it was kind of a joke. At least I thought it was a joke. I was high at the time. On crack. On Chivas Regal, marijuana, and Klonopin, and I thought the whole goddamn thing was a fucking riot, but bankers really don't have a sense of humor. Neither do cops. At least the ones in Pasadena. And, most importantly, neither does my father.

I'd just left my business manager in Glendale, where I'd been in a meeting regarding my trust stuff. Pops was still dishing out a little at a time, but I had learned that day that he'd just made me a $1.2 million profit on a huge position—I couldn't tell you which one. But the dividends that were paid me were being kept, without any hold, in the Pasadena City Bank in the valley. I knew then, after the meeting was over and Ron, my manager, had our joints to smoke after the meeting, that I needed to get that million-two in cash, run off to Vegas with a couple of Mafiosos—"professional baccarat players"—"investment managers, gaming" and win-win-win, then die of crack smoke in my hotel room. This was one of the higher manias I've gone through.

High on crack, I raced down the 134 Freeway in my BMW, doing 120, then tried to turn without slowing down. The car didn't like it, refused to make the turn, and instead went airborne, flying over the divider to the other side, right side up, leaving neither of us hurt seriously. It was a miracle, and I was reborn for half a minute then slid into a blind white fury, jetted up on speed, PCP, and angel dust. I took out some extra Klonopin 4s from my medicine collection—my drive-thru pharmacy in a glove box—to soothe me.

Pulled up to the mini mall and parked.

Inside, nobody was there, only a young woman, a teller. I pulled out my cell phone, leaned across the marble counter, and said in my very best gangster voice, my ego huge from the drugs,

"Listen, we don't want any problem here. I have one point two million here, and I'm a VIP customer, see my driver's license?" I pulled it out.

"The ZIP code . . . nine-one-one-oh-one," I said. "Got it— nine-one-one? And if I press the pound key on this, then . . ."

She said, "Okay, okay, hold on a minute. I'll get you your money."

"Be quick about it then," I told her. "I'm going outside for a smoke. I'll wait."

But she wasn't getting my money—not her—as this happened to be a non-cash bank. To this day, I still don't know what that means—non-cash bank—but what she was doing instead of getting my money was calling the bank CEO, who told her to call the police.

Outside I began to see, not cop cars, but little pins, needle points all around the two-story mini-mall in front of me. Later I found out it was three entire city blocks of police squads and sniper squads, and before I knew it, there were guns and a helicopter and news cameras all pointing at me, all intent on capturing America's Most . . . Stupid: Benjamin J. Schreiber.

"Get down!" I heard.

And I could feel my death right then and there. It started at my feet, crept up my shins, my knees, my thighs. Later I'd find out I was having a reaction to the PCP, but at that point, I was sure I'd been shot, sure I was on my way home to Jesus. (Actually, my mother's Jesus, as I've never been much of a believer myself.)

"Down! Face down. Now!"

I stretched out on the pavement—gingerly; I was wearing Armani. Jesus Christ, what did they expect?

A cop trotted over, gun pointing at my head, and kicked my legs together.

"Ankles crossed, hands spread out! Now."

Now. Now now now. They were all in such a fucking hurry, I couldn't stand it.

"Chill, dude, I'm not going anywhere," I told the air.

Someone I never saw cuffed my ankles together, and then the cop—Sergeant Howitzer (his real name, I swear to God)— yanked me to my feet.

102

Do you know how hard it is to stand upright when your ankles are crossed and cuffed? I fell against the sergeant, my head banging hard against his. It hurt like a son of a bitch. I think I yelped.

The sergeant, not unkindly, righted me. "Son," he said, "you need help."

I'm pretty sure I mumbled something about people telling me that my entire life.

"Maybe it's time you did something about it," he said.

Then he told me that he wasn't arresting me, just detaining me, which made about as much sense as the idea of a non-cash bank, but what the hell.

The only problem—and it was a big problem—was that detaining me included calling my father. My father was neither amused nor unamused; he was simply neutral. Like always. I talked to him at the police station. He was my telephone call.

"Ben," his voice boomed, "how the hell are you?"

"Well, actually," I said, then let the thought drop. I wasn't really sure how I was, and I wasn't all that convinced that my father really wanted to know.

"Yeah, yeah, yeah," my father said. "Heard all about it. Listen, son, I've told Sergeant Howitzer to get you into rehab. Call me once you get settled."

Then he hung up, and Sergeant Howitzer led me out of the station and into his car—a Chevy Malibu, and all I could think was that he needed a BMW. I offered to sell him mine for $5,000. A steal.

"No, thank you," he told me. "I already have a car."

"Piece-of-shit Malibu," I told him.

Funny thing: People—some people, even poor or middle-class people—get attached to their piece-of-shit cars, their piece-of-shit lives. I think I might have insulted him because he cleared his throat once, twice, three times, then kind of snapped at me, "I buy American, son. Always have. Always will."

"Suit yourself," I told him, wondering if my father was paying him to drag me around Pasadena, facility to facility, looking for a place willing to take me. Every single place we stopped was full. After five consecutive facilities are full, you kind of lose your belief that anyone really gives one good goddamn about helping you get better. I think I mentioned it to the sergeant.

"Look, son," he told me. "Don't go getting all paranoid on me. Sometimes a pickle is just a pickle, and sometimes a full-up facility is just a full-up facility."

"Okay," I said, rolled my eyes back in my head, and passed out. When I came to, we were in the parking lot of Valley View Hospital in Sylmar.

How many places did the sarge have to try before he found one that would take me? Out in fucking Sylmar.

But hey, rehab's rehab, and I am nothing if not adaptable when it comes to getting clean. Besides, my nurse Cindy was hot, with super-straight, ash-blonde hair cut to her chin. Looked like the fucking Dutch Boy except with major boobs and curvaceous ass. Fuck.

#

The bureaucrat: it's true, she's your typical lunch lady, obese white woman, rolls of heavy, long breasts and breasts of rolls down her side and front. I take a seat across from her and next to Howitzer. Betty pushes me into the chair across from her and backs away. Obviously, he can smell her belly button gunk as easily as I can, notices her dirty clothes, the mail-ordered scrub set deluxe package, buy-one-get-one-free. She frowns at me and adjusts her scrubs—little happy Smurfs dancing across her boobs. She readjusts her collar, then sticks a cinnamon Altoid in her mouth. You can smell her mold-lubricated tit-sweat as she hadn't washed her clothes too often; once a day seems like once a week. Stinks. The bureaucrat lets out the occasional "silent" pew burp that she passes off as a sigh caused by the late hour, working the ward intake procedures. She's trimmed her moustache and plucked the hairs on her chin, she looks better than she did when she was young and stupid and sick herself, drinking at the community college and telling her college friends that she "wants to help people," her friends all awed by that. And now she's simply not liked by the administration, or by her co-workers, and she's liked least by the poor sickos she takes into the ward. Her sternness is mixed up with a couple of derogatory quips about the others "like us," and she's about as knowledgeable as the books say. I'd imagine that she's real happy in her personal life, but I can't say for sure. Celibate, for sure; at least, that's how she's coming across—not sex-deprived, fucking sexless, could even be hermaphrodite, you know, "intersex," like they prefer to be called now. She reminds me of my mom. She's a pig in scrubs. She's America's finest. She rushes my signing of all the paperwork, not even guessing that I'll read them over in my fucking bedroom, in the psych ward, in this identity-saken heaven . . . in this facility where I'm to stay, where I'm to get better, where I'm to get out, back to the outside world, where I'll be who I am, without restraints if I'm to get out, where I'm to lose any control. I'm still here, inside. You could say I'm in Communist America.

I lay in a cold sweat, wearing all of my clothes—old damp, partly-soiled underwear with piss-drip and loomis, you know— the cheesy discharge from the thigh and underneath thy holy scrotum—sweaty, packed, shriveled, within my oversized blue corduroy pants, my black leather belt taken away by the ward-whores to prevent any suicide action. I wear my sweaty, yellow-stained-white T-shirt underneath my favorite cotton white dress shirt—it's cold on my skin and I'm entangled within it—its buttons are loose, a couple of them broken. The one sheet-like, thin hospital blanket barely covers me, and I'm barely asleep; I keep double-checking with my mind to make sure I really know where I am—but I'm here in the psych ward. The paper-flat, single pillow is far from fluffy and far from keeping its shape— it's too flimsy to fit properly inside its cover, but I've rolled it up, packed my sweatshirt, even some socks and a washcloth, underneath my head to give me some cranial support. It's not like I'm gonna get any other real support here, where I am, for real.

Suddenly, all the dismal fluorescent lights in the room flicker on, and my two other roommates start coughing up their heavy snores. I'm aggravated, but I remember not to lose my lid or to show any anger, frustration, or assertion at all, for any normal reactions to the torture, neglect, and ill-care here—any drama— will cause the hospital techs to gather round me and lock me up in restraints, just like they did last night to one of the anorexic girls, when I had first arrived, because they caught her trying to cut herself with a plastic spoon. She'd sharpened it slightly, but smartly, somehow, with the sizzling heat coming from one of the external pipes in her bathroom. Lucky her that she had any hot water; lucky her, her room had its own semi-private bath. They had to watch her any time she had to pee, or puke—as it was, she wasn't the houseman. He had everything to himself, for he'd been in the ward for a year, the gossip said.

It's five in the morning, and as the lights above flicker on, I'm in a living hell, not prison—a "safer" kind of hell. A loving, beautiful, colorless hell. Childlike crayon paintings on the walls in the activities room. I hate to write about it. They need to take my blood at five in the morning . . .

15. WAX

It's noon, another day, shortly after I met Heide from the gift shop parking lot. I'm obsessing over her while Georgie continues his life with her, with Claudia. I can only imagine what they're up to. I'm all alone in the supermarket parking lot, having a daydream about the mysterious Claudia. How might I find her in my shit life, out of all the women I come in contact with? Georgie, I'm crawling out of my fucking skin!

As I walk inside the market, I notice a cute college co-ed bagging groceries; she gives me the condescending eye, looking like she's up to no good. She's up to something. I pass her off as someone I might hit on . . . some other day. She's cute, and her nametag reads ASHLEY. I start to daydream about Claudia again. . . .

The huge front doors of a vintage luncheonette swing open. Inside, a disheveled, old man is making his rounds from table to table, asking for help. Patrons give him small change. He says, "Thank you."

Georgie sits alone. Claudia walks in, sits alone, a couple of tables away from Georgie. Georgie sees her bruised shoulder near her bra strap. The waitress brings her a cup of joe. Georgie, nonchalantly, moves over. He wants to actualize her, to make her exist. She doesn't seem to mind such a forward attempt from a stranger.

He comments, "You look familiar."

"You say that every time you see me."

"Huh?" says Georgie.

Claudia folds her legs. "Hello? George, it's me! It's Claudia. What's wrong with you?"

Georgie is nervous. "I don't know," he says, as his existence seems to dull a bit. Claudia's stealing it from him. "Okay. You got me," he says.

She leans closer. "I had this guy once . . . I was sitting on a bench in a wax museum, waiting for my friend to catch up and this guy—this total stranger—starts fondling me."

"Fondling," Georgie says, wistful.

"Then I say, 'So what do you think?'"

Georgie starts tapping his feet. "Must have scared him."

"He goes, 'I thought you weren't real.'" Claudia remembers. Georgie laughs. Claudia continues. "I tell him, 'no, they're real all right.' We ended up together for five years."

"Lucky him," Georgie says.

Claudia notices Georgie's small hard-on and asks, "Do you want to sleep with me?"

"Yes."

"You like foreplay?" Claudia asks as she watches George smile shyly.

Later, they're at the beach. Georgie and Claudia sit on the edge of a rock, dangling their feet in the water. Claudia puts her foot in Georgie's lap. He lifts her foot to his mouth.

At the market, they're in the canned food aisle, both in pajamas. Claudia scans the row at eye level. "Do you like pickles?" she asks.

"What?"

"Wake up, Georgie. Pickles. Do you like them?"

"Yeah."

Claudia says, "I like the ones you can get at street fairs, the full sour dill pickles. I can eat them by the jar."

"Me, too," says Georgie.

"So where are you from? Huh? Where are you from?"

Georgie thinks and says, "It's complicated."

"So what brought you here, Georgie? You on the lam? Wanted by the cops?" There's a long pause, then Claudia smiles. "Don't tell me, see if I care." Another moment passes. "Seriously, what brought you here?"

"Termite problem at home. Had to get out."

"Me, too."

Later in the day, Georgie and Claudia are undressing in the Twin Lakes Motel. Georgie bumps Claudia with his elbow. "Sorry," he says.

"Don't be. I'm just glad we could meet so fast and basically get along good."

"I wonder when our first argument will be."

"What it will be," says Claudia. "I wonder if we'll have a falling out."

"Probably," Georgie decides.

"I hope not," Claudia says as she picks out a pickle from the fresh jar of half-sours, store-brand dill pickle slices. "Yeah," she says, "want to practice our break-up now? Tell each other what we really think right this minute?"

Georgie starts. "When we break up, I just want you to know that I'll be dreaming about you. Fantasizing. Even when I'm married."

Claudia scoffs. "Married? You?"

"And I'll despise you. I'll be the guy you hate getting off on you."

Lightly, Claudia says, "You're fucking twisted."

"You're fucking filthy. A whore. A bitch, you easy lay."

"Ooh, you're talking dirty, Georgie. Spank me."

Georgie looks at her triumphantly. "Not if you want me to."

Moments later, they're under the covers, making love.

"What do you want, Georgie? Huh? Little boys? Little girls? The priest himself?" She grinds herself against him. "Come on, baby, tell me. What turns you on?"

"You know. What turns you on."

"I'm stalking you in public, teasing you with thrilling possibilities. Then I make you rape me."

"Why?"

"Because we're both wasted drunk and high."

"Sick. What do you tell yourself about yourself?"

"More fantasies," Claudia admits. "You?"

"That I'm no good."

Just after sex, again, Claudia relieves herself. "I'm sick . . . dizzy."

Georgie laughs.

"Georgie, I didn't understand a word you were saying. All that gibberish. You didn't make any sense."

"I can get like that. Sorry, Claudia."

Claudia looks at him, so sad and alone.

"Oh," Georgie remembers, "by the way, your fee." He pulls a wad of bills from the nightstand. "Four twenty-five, right? You're from LA, Long Beach, wherever, home of cheap sex, cheaper thrills?"

"Yeah, your ten-minute hour is up. Next time pay me before you fuck me," demands Claudia. She smiles. "Do you want me to leave?"

"Why don't I just become your little boy toy? You need that?"

"You already are. Since we kissed on the beach and you fucked me, I've got you hooked. You're already in love with me."

"Yup."

Claudia looks him in the eye. "And yes, I'll marry you."

"The chances of us working out," Georgie says, "are as good as they'd be with anyone else."

"You've got secrets. I've got secrets."

"So no ring then," says Georgie.

"No! That's silly."

"I wish you were real."

I come out of my fantasy and stack up the shopping cart with canned tuna fish. It's funny how the sequence of events has taken its form, in real life and through our inner visions of them separately.

Here's to my incredibly lonely existence.

16. ASHLEY

Service Worker

He knew he should have said "yes" to Ashley, but Georgie failed to come through the day he first met her.

She was sweet and young, blonde highlights in her hair, a cute college coed struggling to get through school and work.

She was there, working the late afternoon shift, bagging groceries. The poor thing was probably thinking about how appetizing all the scanned items looked, how expensive they were and how unhealthy.

"Shit, I need that dish detergent . . . Boy, I could sure go for some cookies 'n' cream . . . Oh, yeah, my bathroom light bulb just blew last night . . . I'm not off again 'til Tuesday."

Her eyes looked up at a forty-five degree angle, like a sad puppy's. Her hand movements were sloppy, but proficient.

Her nametag read: ASHLEY. She was obviously bored. Georgie would have guessed she was single, but he never found out for sure. She no sooner looked him in the eyes with that somber innocence, trying to hide a dirty little smirk underneath her angst.

Georgie stared at her lips. When his eyes drifted up to meet hers for only an instant, he thought, *Uh-oh, caution ahead.*

There were others behind him. He could see from the corners of his glasses.

"Would you like help out to your car?" Ashley asked, with an air of teen elegance. This was a standard procedure at this particular marketplace. They asked everyone. Georgie thought he was special.

He knew the average turnaround was pretty quick for employees at this grocery store. The baggers especially, they tended to float a lot. Adding up the possibilities of what might happen if only he'd say "yes," Georgie bit his lip.

"Well, only if you need a break or something."

"I don't need a break," she suggested. Georgie felt rushed. A long pause haunted the pivotal moment.[35]

"Yeah, um, how about next time? Thanks."[36]

The guy in line behind Georgie would have complained about not having somebody there to bag his things. That's what Georgie thought. Fucking Georgie, who just slammed shut the door to a wide open opportunity, if for nothing but a private walk to his car with Miss Fantasy Girl and an opportunity to flirt, to practice his wit, to test his charm, if for nothing but to experience a small window of time to ask for her phone number in the parking lot.[37]

The guy in line after him was on the verge of calling out in fury, "Hey! This guy doesn't need help out. What the fuck!"

The hell with what Georgie thinks. The other guy was buying a package of diapers for his kid, for Christ's sake.[38]

He feared more problems than promise through any possible exchange of words in the parking lot with Ashley. He would have stuttered, "Heh-heh hey! Can-can can I have your number? Your phone number?"

"Why don't you give me yours, and I'll call you," she'd reply.

The probable mistake of giving away the control factor, the phone number, would have been jaded. He would never get a call from her. Besides, the wall of employee against customer had Georgie tied up in the head through the night.[39]

It would end up haunting him in his already-disturbed sleep that night. A growl full of rage built up deep down in his throat while he continued to dwell on the whole Ashley thing. It was really late. Georgie couldn't sleep one bit.[40]

Ashley no longer does the bagging at the grocery store. She's been promoted to cashier. She still works full-time, and Georgie continues avoiding her.

He takes the express line.

---

[35] *"Answer her already!"*

[36] *"Pussy!"*

[37] *"Georgie, what's wrong with you?"*

[38] *"Life is short."*

[39] *"She was just doing her job."*

[40] *"Admit it. You did not seize the day. Instead, you've avoided it entirely."*

17. LOVE BEYOND DIGNITY

I wake up this morning bombarded with the same intrusive thoughts and obsessions from yesterday. I hasten to think of what today might bring. My alarm clock rings after I've already been awake for ten minutes. I'm still in bed. I let the alarm ring and ring. Its tiny pendulum knocks back and forth against the bell that encapsulates it. Slower and slower, as the batteries inside begin to wear out. I stretch my arms and curl my toes. My eyes are crusty with sleep, and my mouth is dry.

Heading to the sink, the bathroom light extinguishes as soon as I flip the switch on. The noon sunlight squeezes through the blinds of the two small windows to my left. I douse my face with the cold water dispersing out of the sink. I twitch.

I sit on the can and drain myself. I remember the nightmares I encountered just minutes ago. They kept me in bed overtime as I tried to resolve them. But they won me over. I can't remember the details, but I dreamt of another world, someplace I'd never been before. I could feel what, in this world, would be considered happiness and joy. But in the dream, this same bliss was realized as pure misery. All my senses and perceptions existed as their own contradictions. I was with friends, drinking, laughing and playing, but I could see myself as I was dreaming, and I was aware that I was wrong and dishonest and selfish. All the pleasures in my dream life seemed inappropriate. I tried to make them okay, unsuccessfully. I still have an abundance of angst and suffering in my gut, now that I've woken up.

I think of my life now, my real life. Am I a selfish, anti-social narcissist now? Am I delusional now? Are my senses intact? Is everything all right?

I think of lost love, the loss of my childhood and the loss of my life. I think this is a form of depression. It's hard to fathom the thought that I have turned out for the worse. I used to be such a good little kid, happy, bright, and full of life and vigor, dignity.

I head upstairs to my office and start dosing up on joe. I think of what love beyond one's dignity means to me. I've been stuck on this thought for a couple of weeks now, ever since I'd seen the Nicolas Roeg film *Bad Timing*, where Art Garfunkel and

Theresa Russell play two tortured souls involved in a dark and disturbing sexual obsession. Not long after I'd seen this film, I experienced Roman Polanski's outrageous *Bitter Moon*, another study of the dark side of love. I knew I wasn't alone when I saw those films.

I knew I wasn't really all that disturbed.

Stendhal's book, *Love (De L'amour)*, sits on my desk. His notes on the nuances of love and its unfortunate unbalances have me chilled. Even centuries ago, other people were subjected to bad health, even death, because someone wouldn't reciprocate their love, even if only in fictional tales and books.

What has caused this imbalance in me? And why should anybody care? Well, it's worth a shot.

My jealousy continued on Wednesday @ 9:35 AM.

I played Georgie's answering machine at home, having just come back from the drugstore.

"Good morning, Mr. Gust, Miss Nesbitt calling. Hi . . . I didn't want to completely abandon our friendship, wanted to give you a call. I almost called you last night 'cause I was running around cleaning and doing laundry and stuff, but I was kind of on, I was kind of in the zone and didn't want to break up the zone, and I wanted to call and say hello. Just checking in with you to see how you've been and what's going on and what you're going to do for the holidays. I'm probably going to go back east. Anyway, just wanted to stay in touch, and once again, I apologize for amputating myself from your life. It's just, it's just been really, I needed to put 100% into my family, and I'm glad I'm the type of person who can do that with her family, so, anyway, all right, sweetie. Have a beautiful day. I actually just got back from a morning walk, and oh, it's just gorgeous. So that's it. [Her beau's motorcycle starts up in the background.] I'll just catch up with you one of these days. Bye."

I didn't hear from her again as I continued on with my life without her until that Thursday @ 7:31 AM.

"Good morning, Mr. Gust, Ms. Nesbitt here. Just had two seconds and wanted to say good morning and have a beautiful day. I'm always running off and around and about and just wanted to say hello since I'm not the best at returning calls. Take care. I'll catch up with you later. Bye."

116

To Whom It May Concern: It doesn't work to say, "Georgie, don't dwell." I've got an illness, and I hope you can understand that. It hurts me when you tell me what to think or how to feel, because I can't help that. I think that's why we've never had a real, healthy relationship all these years. This is not an attack. It's a realization.

I've been reading up on mental disorders and trying to identify with whatever I can. Part of me, it seems, should just get out of the house, get a regular job, and make friends, but it's easier said than done and there are medical explanations for these "decisions" and my lack of any ability to make decisions and stick to them. A lot of things relate back to past events or situations where I was hurt or taken advantage of. Then fear of trusting others and fears of abandonment and feelings of low self-worth and shame and guilt overwhelm me from there. I'm unable to just "let go" sometimes, and it takes me years to end any given obsession or thought or feeling. That's when I turn internally, resigning to my imagination and fantasy. Reality and the excess of stimuli from the real environment, I can't take them all at once. It's overbearing. It devours me. There's a spectrum of issues I've been dealt.

I continue on my path for meaning and self-discovery.

With Lost Love and Lust . . . and Daydreams,

-Georgie Gust

18. INTERLUDE

A Largo Session

A brilliant largo by Bach, Keyboard Concerto #5 (Largo), plays softly, running for about four minutes, a distraction.

Finally, weird and freaky, he's come to shit on this and so to write since he might try to put it all together, he wrote, playing his own doctor, seeing things and still living in the same nightmare compounded with warps of inescapable terror, hints of mania, genius, pitter-patter, and onslaughts of conduct issues more complex than the new issue of *Hot Tubs*.

He was a lone slut, so pass that heavyweight air biscuit on to the pound dogs, Love.

Let it linger. I like it.

That puppy reeks.

Go fish, go figure alone like a white trash female for ten years slurring speech after ten beers. Brother, you'd think he was anti-social, or a little paranoid, things hadn't taken on any further meanings in his head these days.

He worries, most times, about criticism and takes little or no action to resolve anything, another all-or-nothing ordeal for this girly boy. He sometimes says the whole criticism thing is sadly just a lot of BS, meaning he fears it because he's one to criticize, so it still may be a valid fear, if you get it.

Note: Show off! Don't cut the run-on and gaud! Keep it raw!

He says his name is Dude, and he says Fuck you, you c*** n***** bitch a lot.

Tourette's. Inappropriate language.

He likes large quantities and loves obsessing. Basically, rituals count right in there, too, without a clue of irony and your choice of a pellet of poo or a pornographic violation of his freedom of speech.

He wonders why some things don't make sense. This womanizing gent, attracted to messes and order, ordered chaos and all kinds of bizarre, taboo, fantastic behaviors; he wonders constantly if he might showcase any thoughts into action in the near future.

This guy's full of himself. He likes classical music as opposed to the modern stuff, so call in the K-9s for His Majesty.

He lies most of the time, hoping there's little truth that matters. Those personal, unconventional truths when undisclosed find him embarrassed to a suicidal degree. He's pretty non-social. Not a big fan of clichés or milk, he'll take you up the back with a long sex toy for revealing such matters as, ya know, and he lays out a D-sharp sour down the trombone scales from there fart, bluffing, of course. Talk is cheap as it was. Try that. Then stop.

Stop.

He sees someone through the glass mirror and turns the page of his totally taboo freaks-of-nature magazine. He notices he can mail-order the accompanying videos.

It seems he's trying to find himself through some pitter-patter story he might capitalize on. Again he remarks, you funky-ass bitch, you funky-ass bitch.

Quite tempted to break it up, his racing thoughts, he lets out as effortlessly as an ego-based fictitious situation, "Le-le-lizard," a vocalization. Risk-taking is his favorite pastime.

He rhymes in his head, uses alliteration, sings up there, too. He thinks of excrement, of sex. He fantasizes about love and imagines himself in fucked-up situations, making things even worse than they really are.

This guy's got a secret drawer in his bedroom filled with his unmentionables. He keeps his wallet and checkbooks out in the open.

His thoughts begin to scatter immensely. He starts fingering his unisex poo hole in his sleep and getting fucked up in the head elsewhere by those of the opposite sex. But his body just bloats and grows heavy.

He starts to seem as interesting as someone with a nervous tic.

He's become a gravy-topped queen with garnish, a shrinking little troll, overweight, shriveling. This dude knows they're going to have to do the autopsy on him and bestow a hundred kisses for all his mistakes, when he's able to have a closed mind and open heart. That's fucked up. Go home.

They're still looking at him like fireworks in the sky. Understanding all there is to know about him and how everyone thinks regarding all that they do.

"Forgive me," he begs. "I'm troubled with an array of undisclosed problems of pettiness, a vulgar and obscene mind that breathes the excrement out of flowers. I'm dreaming."

Lighting what you may think are the seeds of a lamb's opium on a bad acid trip, the fire in his mind begins to kindle. He sheds life upon the dead. You wonder where, sex in a graveyard?

Just as cryptically as he falls asleep, everything comes to a circular memory, and the hope for a companion nearly surfaces, wishing for tomorrow, wishing for these days to close. These days, for a second, the attention span alters a lot. Performing a high brow at the tail end, he won't get any scorecards today, I won't get any. No one wins.

Nothing is real now. Reality is an imaginary number. He says they see his balls of steel. But few friends and acquaintances beg to differ, as if there were any.

Who is this guy?

Oh reality, how I dub thee unclear like false shadows of mine.

The guy's just come. He's just gone. He's one of the Shadow People, wearing a little brown cloak, old silver skin, a top notch anti-social. The smartest guy we can imagine, too bad for us. Penis-head shifters and the lasting smell of vaginal look-tar remind him in warp of the slime on a paid-for finger on the way back to a little life.

They dance together in the nude before the hour is up. He and a hooker dance to the sounds of perplexity. Of interest is her rancid smelliness. It's remarkable.

Sipping his coffee and sucking on a cigarette, the Java became His Perplexity: Sweet, strong, black, stale, addictive, and the hooker and he snowball into a passionate lucid love dream with polka-dots and love handles for joy sticks. It doesn't make much sense anymore.

19. CHECKING THE MAIL

It's morning, too early for anyone to be up, not even 9:00, and I stumble out of bed, grab my glasses, pull on a robe, and head down sixteen floors to the mailboxes. It's Tuesday, and I always have mail on Tuesdays—left over from Monday. I never check on Monday, better chance there'll be something there tomorrow, something perhaps from my publisher, who keeps sending back everything I write, usually with cute, coy little notes.

And today is no exception. There, in the back of the mailbox, jammed between a circular for Amazon.com and one for Wanted: Largest Collection of Adult DVDs, is the letter from William & William Publishing. I tear it open in the hallway. Cary's letter flutters to the floor. I bend, pick it up, damn near give myself a hernia—I'm putting on weight these days, going from 160 to 190 then pouncing way up to a diabetic 265, all in the space of six and a half months. I think I'm dying.

Cary's letter is not encouraging:

In a strange way, your short story "Second Skins" makes sense, according to the truth of what really happened, I guess, since our coffee marathon in LA, when you tried to explain everything.

You're quite a handful, Ben. Otherwise, this stuff you've been sending in recently has been point-blank twisted and unnatural, but it makes sense. It's hard to try to think of this as fiction— even for someone who does not know Benjamin Schreiber, it's going to sound autobiographical. The biggest problem with the story is that it casts Georgie as the hero; he isn't even an anti-hero.

That's the problem with Cary Banks: he wants *me* to be a hero or antihero. I'm neither.[41]

---

[41] I'm a thirty-year-old rich kid, living off my father's trust fund, which makes me sympathetic to no one, I know, but the thing is: I don't have any money. My father keeps promising me millions, telling me I'm the richest thirty-year-old unmarried male in the United States, but I've never seen it. It's my father's, and he allocates it when he sees fit, which lately hasn't been too often.

So in the meantime, I sit at home and write or sit at home and try to write or sit at home and obsess or sit at home and wonder why I can't get anything published. The people around me, they tell me I'm the next Bukowski or Burroughs, which means nothing to me. I write what I write, fill it with sex, what I know, what I'm good at, and wait for the go-ahead, wait for the contract. So far, I've been waiting a year and a half. That's forty-three chapters, 92,322 words, mostly about Heidi, or rather mostly about Claudia as seen by Georgie.

Dr. C said by our second session that I've got a problem with obsessive thinking.

"No shit," I blurted back to her.

She also said Georgie's not a real character, that he's nothing more than an alter ego, infused with all the feelings that I refuse to feel, and that when I get healthy, Georgie will simply die an appropriate death, and I can move on with my life.

Whoever said I wanted to move on?

20. MOTHER'S NAKED FRIEND

For the past three months, I have seen Dr. C every Monday and Wednesday promptly at 3:30. I like seeing her on the half hour. It's odd. Unique. Peculiar. *Peculiar*: Good word.

I like that I'm peculiar. In fact, I have elevated peculiarity into an art form, from the way I dress (oversized hats and glasses, Hugo Boss loafers, never any socks)—to what I eat (strictly raw, I never cook anything)—to my sex partners (I like them old). The older the better. Which is why Dr. C, even with her slingback, open-toed, fuck-me sandals and electric blue toenails, doesn't turn me on. Too young. She's just too young. As far as I'm concerned, a woman under forty is still half-formed.

My fascination with older women started early, right around the time my parents got divorced. Right about the time I saw Darlene Krokus naked.

Darlene was my mother's one and only New Jersey friend and was around all the time after Pops left—for dinner, canasta, and from three to five every Thursday afternoon immediately following my mother's weekly Weight Watchers meeting. My mother was a Weight Watchers failure. Not only did she not lose weight, but she actually gained. Ostensibly my mother gained weight due to her glandular problem, but in reality she gained weight due to Darlene's love of hot fudge brownie sundaes, complete with whipped cream, nuts, and maraschino cherries.

Even at twelve, I knew that nobody could lose weight eating hot fudge, brownie sundaes, but Darlene had Moms convinced that these were special 'negative calorie' sundaes that would actually burn calories and help her lose weight. A lot like exercise. Moms was never overly bright, and after Pops left, she believed what she wanted, no matter how asinine. She refused to see the connection between the food she crammed down her throat and the number—that magical number—on the scale. Up and down, down and up. Up, up, up.

Moms was a big woman back then—bigger now, I'm sure—but still pretty hefty back then. And with Darlene's help, she got even heftier. Darlene, unlike Moms and Moms' other friend,

125

Debbie Sedgewick, was a Weight Watchers success. Fit and trim. Both Moms and Debbie idolized her, wanted to be just like her, and would do anything Darlene told them to do, including eating those 'negative calorie' sundaes and playing racquetball at the Tenth Street Gym.

The thing with my mother is that she never exercised. Never. Even getting out of bed in the morning was too strenuous for my mother. If she'd had her way, she'd have had assistants who'd roll her straight from her bed to a gurney and then roll her downstairs to the kitchen, her coffee, and her Pop-Tarts, and then on down the hall to the living room and straight to her overstuffed chair and her omnipresent TV.

However, with Darlene, my mother was a different woman— motivated to at least pretend she knew how to exercise, so off she'd go once or twice a week to the Tenth Street Gym and pretend she wanted to play racquetball. In reality, my mother always found an excuse not to play: one week, she had gout, another week, she had a goiter, and once, for an entire month, she had pernicious anemia that left her light-headed and much too weak to do anything but stay in the house. (I suspect that Moms is the reason I have such trouble with my own hypochondria.) And when she ran out of diseases, my mother relied on me—and my 'disorder'—to keep her off the racquetball court.

. . . Which is how I ended up seeing Darlene Krokus naked.

My mother had already used up her gout and goiter excuses, hadn't yet discovered the pernicious anemia excuse, so had dragged me along to explain why she couldn't play yet again.

A tanned and toned Darlene, dressed in white shorts and matching knit shirt, met us in the lobby of the Tenth Street Gym, kissed the air on either side of my mother's face and ruffled my hair.

"Oh, Rose," Darlene trilled, "he's getting soooo biiig."

I blushed appropriately and scuffed my toes against the tiled floor.

"And sooooo handsome," she said.

"Still a handful though," Moms said. "In fact, Dar, that's why I have to sit this one out. Benjy got himself kicked out of school again."

126

Moms rolled her eyes.

"The tics," she said. "They just don't understand them."

"Oh, poor Benjy," Darlene said.

I blushed.

My mother massaged the base of my neck, like she loved me or something, and told Darlene she'd meet up with her after racquetball.

Darlene beamed. "Absotively, Rose."

My mother then marched me off to the women's locker room, so she could weigh herself.

Okay, now—nearly twenty years later—I wonder about my mother's motivation. I was twelve. I didn't need to be with her every minute, and I certainly didn't need to be in the women's locker room, but that was my mother: a woman I'm still trying to figure out.

When I was twelve, I was sure her motivation was to humiliate me, and I fought back. Maybe I couldn't keep her from parading me and my Tourette's out in front of her friends, and maybe I couldn't keep her from dragging me into the women's locker room, but I could keep her from weighing herself in private. In fact, I delighted in keeping her from weighing herself.

My mother's weight has always been a carefully guarded secret. On her driver's license, she admits to 150, which she hasn't weighed since she was twelve. Like I said, my mother was and is a hefty woman.

My mother, her hand still gripping my neck, pulled me with her into the locker room, pushed me down on the bench, and told me not to move.

"Sure, Moms," I said and promptly grimaced at her—one of my favorite tics and one I could perform on command.

"And stop doing that," she told me.

"Okay," I said, then blinked and wrapped my right arm over my head and scratched my left ear.

My mother hurried away. I waited half a second, then snuck off after her, ducking in between the benches and rows of lockers, intent on finding out how much she weighed. It was something I was always trying to do, even back at the house. I'd pretend I had horrible, explosive diarrhea and was just about to let loose unless she let me into the bathroom with her. Right then. At that precise moment. Once I actually pushed open the door, burst in on her—her and her scale—tried to sneak a peek at it, but my mother shrieked, jumped off the scale, and all I saw was the needle bouncing: back and forth, forth and back.

So that day in the locker room, I was intent on finding my mother, discovering what she weighed. In fact, I was so intent, so focused, I almost but not quite—not quite by a long shot actually—failed to realize that Darlene Krokus, in all her naked beauty, was standing directly in front of me, completely nude.

I'd been ducking in between benches and the endless rows of lockers, turned a corner, and came upon her: Darlene Krokus in her glory. Breasts and pubes uncovered. She was magnificent.

Her breasts—they were gorgeous—flat with dark, prominent nipples. They took my breath away and made my dingdong go straight up, made my little general stand at attention. I loved them, wanted to put my little twelve-year-old hands all over them. Fondle them. Molest them. Yet, as wonderful as those breasts were, they couldn't compare with her snatch. Her pubes. Hairy. Perfect V-shaped patch. It made my mouth water. I stood there gawking at Darlene, who stood there talking to my mother's other friend, fat Debbie Sedgewick.

Finally, Darlene must have felt my presence, and she turned, caught my eye with hers and smiled. Seductively. Invitingly. Then glanced at the bulge in my pants.

"Enjoying the show?" she asked, then pulled her clothes on exquisitely, methodically, torturously slowly—all the while staring straight at me.

What a glorious four months that woman gave me—four months of unmitigated jerk-off pleasure.

When I tell Dr C about my thing for older women and when it started, she doesn't say anything, just kind of wrinkles her mouth, shows her crooked tooth, and raises her eyebrows. She drives me crazy wondering what she's thinking.

Then I tell her more about Georgie and how my thing for older women is something he shares. Age is so relevant in Georgie's life. He's fascinated with age. It is, however, one of the only things we share because Georgie is not me. He doesn't even look like me. I look like a rock star. A young David Bowie or Simon Le Bon. I'm hot. I wear Hugo Boss loafers, no socks.

Armani jeans. Still, I'd rather be who I am than who Georgie is. Every day, all day long, Georgie does nothing. Doesn't change, doesn't move. Nothing does.

#

Georgie's feet are a size twelve, and he wears shoes all the time. His feet embarrass him. He has a foot fetish. He wears blue shoes.

His legs are still in shape, but he wears long pants no matter how hot the weather gets. His legs embarrass him, too. Otherwise, he's your generic overweight pumpkin.

His plump belly sticks out. Maybe it's cute and huggy-bearish to some single sex addicts, but hell if Georgie thinks so. He's addicted, too. He weighs in around 260. His driver's license says he's 168. The picture doesn't even look like him, but the photo came out pretty nice.

He used to be in shape.[42]

His passport picture is pleasing. He enjoys looking at images of himself.[43]

---

[42] Now he just recites affirmations.

[43] Dr. C tells me this is revealing—that Georgie likes looking at images of himself—and asks if I like looking at images of myself; after all, I'm skinnier. I sidestep, ask why she's asking. "Do you think I might be narcissistically wounded?" I ask her. "Is that it?" She says nothing, and I am persistent, ask her on which axis of the DSM-IV she'd place me. She smiles, but not like she's happy, and says, "And on which axis would you place yourself, Ben?" "Depends on the day," I tell her, "the weather, whether I've gotten laid. I'm being a smartass, I know, and if my mother were around . . ."

21. MOTHER AND HER LAVA SOAP

When my mother wasn't parading me out in front of her friends, making me twitch on command, she was yelling at me for being a smart ass, for having Tourette's, grooming my life experience as if preparing me for the borderline personality disorder I'd resent later in life, if I'd even known what that meant.

I'd feel an exaggerated emptiness, most likely later on in life, and act out according to a disturbed ring of emotions. I must still be this wounded kid. I can still recall every precise detail of Moms and her domination over me.

"You think just because you've got some sort of fucking disorder, I'm going to let you talk to me like that," she'd shriek.

And then she'd swat me on top of the head with a rolled-up newspaper like she thought I was some sort of two-legged dog.

I hated my mother growing up, and I know—I think—that's probably a horrible thing to admit, but I couldn't cope with the woman. I had Tourette's; it made me swear. I couldn't help it, I couldn't fucking help it, but she didn't seem to really care. This was so confusing to me. When she wasn't swatting me with the newspaper, she was washing my mouth out with soap. And, yes, I know lots of mothers wash their kids' mouths out with soap, but my mother washed mine with Lava Soap. Even now, twenty years later, I still have the taste of pumice in my mouth.

Now, now that I'm therapy again, dredging up the past, looking for answers, I wonder if all that pumice somehow got me thinking about women's feet and left me with such a peculiar fetish.

Dr. C said early on that a foot fetish is not peculiar and is, quite the opposite, common in men like me.

"Like me?" I asked, looking away from her, at some silly calendar on the wall.

She stammered, stuttered. I turned my eyes back at her, a ribbon of saliva dripped from the corner of her mouth, and for a minute she looked so goddamn imperfect, it was all I could do not to throw her on the ground and fucking attack her, but then she cleared her throat, smiled, and said, "Men like you, Ben. Men with self-esteem problems."

Self-esteem problems? I know I have self-esteem problems, which is probably the reason I love feet.[44]

---

[44] *Dr. C's Session Notes* 10/11/06: Pt. was late. Arrived at 3:45 for 3:30 appointment. Focused as to time, date, name criteria. Discussed medication options. 10/16/06: Pt. non-communicative. Left at 4:05. 10/18/06: Pt. states that he suffers from schizophrenia. (?) states Georgie Gust is literary device not individuated personality. 10/23/06: Pt. states mother cause of foot fetish, story of the first time he saw naked woman (m's friend: Darlene K.) Provisional diagnosis: PTSD. Possible etiology: Maternal sexual contact (?)

22. A VALENTINE REMINDER

It's Valentine's Day.

I get in my car. A little hatchback I've had forever. I barely drive it, but I need to get out of the house. It's damn lonely being single sometimes, especially on this holiday.

So I celebrate myself. I ponder on what could have been with Marilyn. I don't give her enough time in my head obsessing. I owe her.

I drive down the Pacific coast. Traffic is safer there than on the freeways. But before long I grow bored and head back home. I'm a little sad, a little wimpy and pathetic.

I remember my last break-up. Back when I was immature, impulsive, and horny. I didn't break up with Marilyn. She broke up with me. It's been a while.

I hardly ever answer the phone. That's what voicemail's for. I remember. I was in a pissy mood all morning. Marilyn owed me a call. I shut the ringer off.

"Hey, it's Marilyn. It's Friday, and it's around five o'clock or so, I think. I'm home. I'm going to be home the next couple of hours, so if you get this in time, give me a call. I'm sorry I didn't call last night, but you can call me today."

I opened a fresh pack of smokes and lit up, gripping the portable phone, dialing back. I remember her kitchen.

She lived a couple of hours away. I used to take the train to see her. She was a fuckin' animal. So was I; we were sexaholics.

From our initial blind date, I brought Marilyn back home with me. When she spoke openly of her frustration through menopause, my roommate at the time knew something was off.

"Isn't she a little old for you?" he suggested.

But my roommate was a little weird himself. He liked his girls young, real young, all-too-fucking young. Fuckin' pedophile.

Marilyn had stretch marks. For some odd reason, they attracted me. She had those old-lady nipples. She couldn't have kids, and she was loyal. No rubbers were needed.

The phone rang once. "Hello?" I answered.

"Hi."

"How are you?"

"Great."

"Good."

. . . Typical Americans.

"So what's happening?" I asked Marilyn.

"Oh, I'm just eating, some vegetable soup, some tea. I wanted to talk, if you had time," she said candidly.

Then she broke up with me—funny, it wasn't due to my age.

"I don't want to put the blame on you," she said, "it's not something that you'd be able to solve. You need someone more attractive and around, and very, very into you."

"No regrets. No hard feelings," I told her.

There was a long silence. No one tried to break it for a several moments.

"So, do you have another man in your life now?" I asked politely.

"No. The thing is . . . that's surprising. There's always got to be someone and you assume that if I'm not with you, then there must be someone else. I'm just really independent."

"What went wrong?" I asked her. "Were you uncomfortable with me?"

"No. I don't necessarily . . . I mean I'll tell you this, but I think I'm a really low-maintenance person. I think you're kind of high maintenance. You need to know from me, always, that everything is all right. You have a constant need for reassurance. But I think how you were so honest with me and that was so important to me. You always asked how I was feeling. I just can't deal with that high maintenance."

"What should I work on? I mean I'm not going to change."

"No," she said, "don't change! Again, there's your need for reassurance. Listen, I'm pretty free-ended. I hope you're not lonely."

I immediately changed the topic.

I love The Talk women often engage in if you request such an analysis of what really happened. You can find out your weak points and your strengths before you cease to lay your eyes on her ever again, just as she's becoming your ex. You learn more about how the other species relates to you. You learn not just what a dick you really are, but how your unworthiness has

134

actually become apparent. I tend to get a clearer picture of who I am and what a piece of work I can be for women to deal with.

But nothing has stopped me yet from pursuing love, whether it's true love or not. I keep trudging along, even through the storms. There's some huge void in my life I've got to fill. I've got to figure some things out.

Valentine's Day is over now. There's always some promise for next year.

Perhaps, by then, I'll be a little different.

23. FUNERAL

I think of my petty little funeral. I lie in the overpriced coffin, fully insulated, wondering what all the others are up to. Maybe I'm just a little angry. I cried myself to sleep last night as it was. Like a little baby. Like a loser. I hear all the women I've ever been with speak their minds. They comment on what kind of lover I was . . .

"He was fine, I mean he was all right. He was really sweet and really cute."

"He was really funny."

It's Judgment Day.

"There were so many times we would have these intense conversations, all this philosophy stuff, and he would just go off and lose his shit and I'd just sit there and be completely confused and start crying."

"I never knew completely what was going on in his head."

"I think that's what I loved about him the most, though, his complexity. I couldn't grow bored with him easily."

I think of all the other broken hearts that have lived throughout time. They had so much passion, but their lives probably felt so dull. Their passion wasn't produced. It welled up inside them until the end.

There's so much brilliance, work, art, diatribes, subtle moments of supreme happiness, legendary artifacts buried in basements, epic beauty, manuscripts in the trash, throughout the history of mankind. I try to feel important. I'm surrounded by nature. I'm not sure what it is I'm still looking for.

The women still whisper in succession.

"I was always curious as to what was going to happen next."

I hear music, a Bach death march versus Led Zeppelin, divided by Culture Club. I try to translate all that I hear into a personal love story, but all I want to do is to die.

My funeral is held at a crack house.

The women of my dreams shared moments of true happiness with me. They're now merely delusions.

"Was there really anybody even there?" I gasp.

I try to stay alive and keep the faith.

I'm out at the bar late, giving into temptation.

"You've worried me in the last twenty-four hours."

She stayed with me when my car overheated in the rain. I want to remember this. Remember her.

"Move on."

"Change, reduce the bad stuff, the rage, the blaming, the spoiled boyishness, the lying, the violent thoughts."

I tried to try before it was too late. I failed to commit and follow through fully.

She slid my hand away the moment I made her cum with my fingers. I made love with a live person. I was in the moment. The moment's gone.

I lied. They lied.

I broke up with another woman this morning. Melanie.

I had no self-respect, for the last time, at last. It was finally over. All the chaos, it was over.

I remember tearing up when the two of us made love for the first time. I thought no one else would know.

Melanie was The One.

During the procession, traffic's a mess. Fear sinks in.

"Am I still alive?" I can't tell. I seemed to have separated from myself. I question the news helicopters above. I'm stuck in self. I've become a complete narcissist, completely delusional. Yet I still feel like something's incomplete. Claudia . . . I remember Claudia more than anyone.

The copters fly like locusts, weaving back and forth, taking out everyone on the freeway with machine guns and rocket launchers. I'm the only one to escape. The whole city is a parking lot, a massacre, a graveyard. I'm lost. The whispers still linger in my head.

"I welcomed you into my home, felt drawn to you and your loneliness."

I held hands with her for the first time. It's never felt the same again. I never forgot the feelings of things happening. I felt cheated, but I wasn't.

"I don't think that either of us used each other."

"It was a warm and loving exchange between two shattered souls."

"I'll save you. You save me."

138

I pray to be corrected. I'm meeting myself through the help of others who once fulfilled my life.

"You're a very intense man, and I am much too delicate to deal with all of you."

"When will you be ready?" I asked.

Memories I've saved throughout the years, they have such a profound impact on me. I think, *Who am I? Who was I?*

"It's been almost three weeks since I've seen you, and I hope you were able to maintain your goal. I must say, however, your absence from the bar is a positive sign."

"You ran like a madman into the drugstore to get me an aspirin when I had that extraordinary headache."

"You opened up and cried your pain to me. You made me laugh."

"You were loving to my animals, and you didn't complain when Candy and Lolly's fur made you all stuffed up."

"You ate my Thanksgiving dinner. You asked for seconds."

"You said, 'Thank you.'"

"You held me. You held my hand when we walked. You gave that bum two dollars for bringing back my necklace when it fell off."

"You cleaned your bathrooms before I came over."

"You said to me, 'You were the most beautiful in that bathtub.'" It was so beautiful. There's beauty in conflict, too. In despair, things take on a new meaning.

"But you are so many harsh and unforgiving things and mostly to yourself."

"Part of growing up is taking responsibility for what we do. Stop blaming everybody else. It's hard enough to be a parent to somebody without issues. They did the best they could. They didn't cause anything wrong."

"So, take care."

"I miss you."

"I just wanted to hear your voice."

"Whenever you need me . . ."

"You respected when I asked you not to call, and you didn't."

"Nobody is holding a gun to your head but you."

"Might you find the love and strength inside yourself, the love that I have witnessed and been grateful to receive, might you make some realizations and take control of your life in a loving, healthy way and, like I said, make some goddamn changes, positive changes?"

"I am leaving you."

"You have hurt me profoundly."

"Verbal abuse, alcohol, yelling, gambling, harsh criticisms, humiliation, disdain."

"In your good days, you were definitely more affectionate than usual."

"You opened doors for me. You said things like, 'This is your night.'"

"You are the only person I know who truly made me feel like a woman. Nobody else has yet."

"I have confidence in myself from you."

"But you made me feel more miserable than happy."

"Do this. Do that."

"You called me 'bitch,' even when we were most intimately together."

"You farted on me. I couldn't believe it!"

"But inside you're a sensitive and tender gentleman. Where did that man go?"

"I just hope that the pain, sorrow, and bitterness will eventually fade away for both of us."

"Please let me know what you decide to do."

Very important detail: I didn't know what I was doing! Blind ambition captivated my every thought and action. I dissolved. I made my dwelling in solitude. I would acquire what I could personally. My character remains the same. Strange and bizarre thinking, mental disturbances caused my mind to suffocate. I withdrew from reality the best I knew how.

I'm still addicted to Melanie. I love a woman who can't love me. She's got a lot of baggage. A lot like me. I thought she was all right. I guess I've changed a little. So what did she have to say about us?

"We're two different people. But I'm not going anywhere."

I'm doing my best to just forget about her all day long. I begin with some kind of ending. I require detail and important facts, truths that elicit positive emotions.

I think about how love can't always be rushed. Love at first sight, true love. They're lies. But I'm attracted to them. I dive into a bag of chips and buy some smokes and a small lighter at the counter. I pay with my check card. Caffeine, smokes, Slush Puppies, dreams of purple Pez—they're a little hard to find these days. A little like happiness.

In the end, I wondered what all this meant. I let these echoes help create a better man in me. I'm not alone. I'm still here. I move on the best that I can. Things tend to get a little better during these short detours we have in our minds. We change. I change. I celebrate. I improve myself. It's like a broken-hearted jubilee.

Shit, I'm out of milk and sugar, and the coffee's almost done brewing. It's damn past one in the morning, and I require amplification. The supermarket's open late, really late. Got to head over there now. Perhaps I'll decide to pick out some point-of-purchase items on display by the checkout line, like a pack of chewing gum or a packet of Triple-A batteries to store in the freezer.

Georgie needs a light bulb for over his desk.

I need a night light to plug into the bathroom wall.

I need to write another list.

What else? Another set of scattered thoughts . . .

24. "WASTE"

Notes on Ben's Novel

Frustrated with having so much to say about something so simple, the words in my head have turned to salad. It would seem that the real problem involves a year-long obsession with Claudia. Or Heidi. Both of them. Perhaps it was love at first sight with my Heidi causing me to admit all that has happened between Georgie and his Claudia, to express the details of my obsession with this perplexing idea and what it has caused. Things have really blown out of proportion.

Claudia was the prototype of my dream woman. Even after we'd separated, she'd continued to haunt me as a real flesh-and-blood person, further infesting my otherwise incredibly lonely and desperate existence. Ever since Claudia found her way into my life and love was born, I decided to sober up in order to become a better person for her in case I ever saw her again. But instead of lifting the fog and confusion in my mind, life without alcohol and drugs has only added to my perplexed state. I blamed my overwhelming mental condition on the incompleteness of my relationship with Claudia.

Meanwhile, my impotence to succeed in life, a better life, mind you, takes second place. Besides, I already had everything I needed. I had one desire, I thought—that Claudia would interact with me full-time. But because she's no longer around, all sorts of fantasies, both haunting and exhilarating, have taken up residence in my dreadful little mind. Like right now, I'm sinking.

I'd write a pastiche in the present tense, but it's all happened at different times. I can't think. I leave my existence behind. The lights dim. All is quiet. The sky is gray, flat, and still. The rain falls without a pause, absolute silence. Watching the clock, I wait for tomorrow. I throw my pack of cigarettes away. I'm no brilliant demagogue. I'm an aberration, a misconception, a miscreant. Boy, these anti-depressants don't do shit. My vision's getting murdered, going blind-like, finally. My sense of sight was diseased as it was, for the very sight of Claudia was like seeing the Devil face-to-face. It's nighttime, time to get to sleep. I stay up and write. My imagination's on fire.

I think I see Claudia everywhere, someone I want but can't have. God, I'm just a waste of sperm and egg. What's gotten into me? Lord, hear our prayer! And Claudia? I'm sick over you. And Heidi? *Hmph!* . . . I've tried, and I've failed to achieve all that I've wished for. I tic. I take a tack and prick my skin, realizing that nothing I experience can be expressed in words. Everything remains as thoughts as if all that I sense is secret. So, I lie. Listen to me mumble like a mouth full of marbles! "Claudia!"

Claudia . . . Claudia . . . What a shite mess-like! I'm not even Irish. I look on in wonder at the mess I've created. I'm still alive. That's about all. I need to finish what Claudia and I started on the miraculous day I made my pathetic little trip to the convenience store and had my encounter with her. Everything seems a little dreamy. Dreams aren't any more significant than our thoughts. I think every day, the same repetitive things. But these things confuse me. My dreams don't confuse me as much as my thoughts.

Georgie and Claudia muddle in with the environment.

"I love you," Georgie tells her as he dissolves into a deep slumber.

Maybe there is no more sex with that woman, Georgie thinks to himself. *Have I just realized this?*

I watch Georgie scoff with intent, switching off the bathroom light, leaving only the light coming in from underneath the door. A mental parade of people can be seen hovering over his head. They wear halos. "They must be looking over me, like angels. They're looking after me. That's it," Georgie concludes and steps out in his cloth robe. "I've got to get back home, but I don't want to go."

Checkout was at noon.

#

It's two in the afternoon, and Georgie is now home. He'd spent the night at the local hotel because geographical change is the easiest quick-fix when stifled by too much stress and heartache. Georgie's reclined on his reading chair, facing the white wall in his bedroom. He's still reflecting on the strange episode at the hotel. He stands up and draws the window shade down and thinks, *But who's possessing whom? What's going on here?*

A while later, Bobby Banks calls him up. Georgie forgot he had any friends. Typical American: "Hello . . . What are you up to?" etc.

"Hey, are you still fucking around with that chick next door? Claudia, right?" Bobby finally asks.

I haven't spoken to my best friend since high school, Georgie thinks. *Ten years. He came out to visit me last year, and we've kept in touch ever since. He seems to care.*

I'm fast asleep in dreamland. His alarm clock is shut off on the nightstand.

Georgie and Claudia . . . and my mindless attempt to complicate things because that's what my mind does. That's what Georgie's mind does.

I feel like a character in a B movie, like a badly written character in a crap-stinking Movie-of-the-Week. I'm so fed up and tired. I'm finished. I'm through.

"Keep trudging along, you're not gonna die anytime soon, so quit bitching," I hear Georgie yell. I yell it back to him.

The doctors advised me last week about the importance of "my meds." They said, "Remember your meds . . ." I remember how I miss my sanity when I'm off them. I feel like such a stereotype; I feel like I'm nothing exciting, nothing important, like I'm not being prepared for anything.

In my new home in Los Angeles (I finally moved here from Manhattan, then Pasadena; it took four truckloads) anyway, the "sober hallucination" of Georgie Gust was more vivid than ever, frightening me. Soon, our new neighbor, Claudia Nesbitt, would take up a new residence in Georgie's mind. I could sense her existence. She was beautiful, however uncommonly you want to believe. Fuck it; she was perfect. However, Claudia was a chaotic woman at the same time. The idea of her excited me and my imagination. She still does to this day. And that's that.

Georgie's sensual affair with Claudia, in turn, has shattered the entire heart and soul of the very man who tried to replace Heidi with Claudia.

Jump inside one of our heads for about five minutes. Never a dull moment up here.

Thank you.

To the reader, looking back, with love,

-Ben.

#

I'll take a hop, skip, and a jump to the present moment, looking back, always.

25. PORTA-POTTY

When you've got to take a shit, they say, when you gotta go, you gotta go. Georgie and I are packing up. We're moving out of town, running away. We're going to leave some brutal and bittersweet memories behind, from every window of our dumpy, little abode across the street from Claudia Nesbitt's tiny, one-bedroom paradise.

Whatever we could see inside and out, we're leaving it all where it will now stay, buried in the past, the cemetery of yesterday.

Some people say that yesterday is today. Tomorrow is today. Today is no longer. We tend to think along the same lines, Georgie and me.

Georgie left a message on Claudia's voicemail: "Would you like to take a walk with me? To see the sunset?"

No answer. Claudia no longer speaks to him.

Sometimes he'll see her outside, on her way out, on her way in, while I'd stay in, writing about the things I see Georgie do. Feeling what he feels, for the most part.

Claudia Nesbitt. She's turned into such a cold hag. She's still the most problematically beautiful woman Georgie's ever laid eyes on. I still wish I could see her.

Georgie will give his creation redeeming qualities when he deems them appropriate. He wants to change her to suit himself.

As the author, I have a tendency to sit around brooding on what could have been with my muse, another woman resembling Claudia Nesbitt in so many ways.

Heidi Berillo.

I brood on the possibilities of what could have been between us. What we could have been like together, if we had kept in touch.

Georgie is a lot like me, and his idea of Claudia is a lot like that of my Claudia. She's real. Georgie and his girl are certainly not. They're both beautiful, basically.

Beautiful, such a generic term, so clichéd, a little like life itself. What poetry! If I can't try to be poetic, much less pull it off, I've still got a little charm left. I think.

Georgie writes in his journal, "She kidnapped my heart and soul and while she's holding them hostage, I can't breathe."

I've been sober a while now, and there's no more need for fogginess. I've got to learn to be lonely without losing my mind. I'm not sure how this might happen. How I might lose Georgie by choice. How I might move on.

I obsessed over him so he'd obsess for me. Taking one poor woman and creating the ultimate Perplexity.

We've been through all that was necessary together. Things were too out of hand. Just the two of us, submitting ourselves to a sick seduction by the oh-so-familiar third wheel, my Claudia with me, Georgie with me and Claudia Nesbitt, the woman of my daydreams and Georgie's real life. Three relationships. Our unity was my secret, Georgie and me. It was what we kept to ourselves.

I want Georgie's girl. I want my very own Claudia. A Perplexity I can actually deal with and feel a loving connection to. Oh, baby, with your pretty face. Ms. Nesbitt was too busy sipping her bottle of sake and getting her nails done professionally to satisfy Georgie's needs. He enjoyed painting her toes. I would have otherwise taken such satisfying delight maintaining her pedicures. I think of the colors of choice: Adolescent Pink, Hooker Blue, Metallic White, Purple Plus, Silver and Sparkles.

I would show her love if she was mine. I'd spoil her with compliments and presents. Give her foot massages and pedicures.

She stepped on me with her feet instead, smothering my soul, biting my thighs like she used to.

Georgie would have to make this happen for me. Bite her thighs.

I'd like to really piss her off. Fucking bone her with a rabid tampon. Boy, what the hell's gotten into me? I'm angry. I'm really fucking angry right now.

Georgie is a product of what I produce on paper. But it was Claudia's sinfully beautiful girlfriend, Sara, lush doctor of pain from the flats of Beverly Hills, who bit Claudia's thighs. Georgie noticed the bruises she left by her crew-cut crotch. He finally confirmed the sadist biter's identity with Claudia when coming home from one romantic evening with her during the better days, the early days. He ended up revealing her passion for teeth to me another night.

I was looking across the way where Georgie had known his Perplexity lived and slept. Her lights would go out each night at ten minutes to twelve. I could never see her. I was aware that some woman lived in the apartment across the way, but I could never see her face, her identity. I couldn't carry on any dialogue with our complex neighbor due to an equally baffling situational warp probably caused by our years of smoking angel dust and rock cocaine, cigarettes dipped in PCP, bottles of red wine, and Goldschläger.

Claudia's thighs were bruised by somebody else, someone not real in my world. But Georgie felt all the due envy and lack of true possession in his own world of someone he seemed to love, too, someone who couldn't love him back. Her character was inferior to the heightened rank of Georgie's personality. Georgie's feelings were sometimes passed on to me. Georgie is as real to me as I am to myself. I wonder what I am to him.

Scratching Georgie's back with her fingernails and leaving temporary scars he wished would stay there forever, Claudia invited temptation. Her deep voice carried an air of thrill and danger and fun. And fun is good. But she often wouldn't follow through with her invitations to have a good time together. There was a lack of control. Her life wreaked havoc.

She was perfect in the beginning, just like the Claudia I met on my way to get smokes one morning. Poor her, she's unaware of the influence she has had on my senses. She's essentially the mother of Georgie and his version of our Claudia, someone sexy and wild and sadistic. Loveable and prone to be an obsession.

Sex for Claudia was lovemaking to Georgie. She'd whisper, "Georgie, Georgie," from her first-story bedroom, clutching the portable phone with Georgie on the other end.

"I miss you. I've missed you."

"Leave a message and I'll call you back."

Look who's talking? Look who's listening. "Look at my baby's cute little haircut! It feels so soft. You smell so good."

Once Georgie and I made a deal that we'd work as a team, our Perplexity became an obsession we'll never fully forget, a full fantasy, a partial reality.

At first, we had her. She had us. We had each other. It was thrilling until we let her go, through the fault of others' influences and that of our own. We got her back. Then we fell into her trap of control. She manipulated us like tricks. She used us as her very own personal nemesis. Georgie was trapped in the bewilderment she bred. I looked on, letting her enrapture two hearts and one mind.

She upheld her self-redeeming fantastic appeal, and we slaves needn't but worshiped all that she wished for and that which she didn't even want in the first place.

We were stuck until I finally found a way to interact with the ultimate Perplexity, the day Georgie told me about the day she blew his head off in the studio via Claudia, an alter ego of the she-devil herself.

The tables turned, and I was able to write my way into Georgie's mind and take his creation for myself. But she would make me unhappy. She would cause a sensual obsession. She would cause my horrible loneliness to be complemented by ideals both beautiful and bovine. I continue to live for Claudia's chaos and the cozy catastrophe she leaves in her wake wherever she goes.

My muse is no longer here to show me how she complements her beyond that about her which I already know.

It's pertinent that I explain all this colorless confusion, this semi-controlled craziness, this schizoaffective situation, but, simply said, what I see is not clear, so we should all probably just put our minds to rest and leave each other alone. Aside from that, I want to fall in love and take care of someone else, not myself. I want to be faithful. I want to do everything anybody I've ever come into contact with is incapable of doing.

Those people, "The Others," this Honda Generation, the Totally Young Generation, these modernists include the people I have no relation to. Should I need to sneak my way into this secret society, give me love first, then I'll conform but hate myself. I'm just another normie, basically. A normal person, nothing special. I must be too hard on myself. Those I hallucinate have hallucinations of their own. I wish things were simpler. I swim around in this little fish pond of my day, of my own miniature world. I try to become a hallucination myself, driving myself up the wall and lighting a cigarette.

I want another heart attack. I need to give up my self-destructive thoughts soon. The clock ticks, tics, tics, tics. Because of the sexual agony she caused, Georgie and I had to sink ourselves into our selves. We had to look inside, and inside was warm. We wanted her. I wanted her more than anyone. What an idea!

"I know you do, but not tonight, Georgie." Her bossy side came out.

I still held on to the idea of her. She held on to Georgie. White flags went up. Green flags followed. The months would pass with a pure stop-and-go play routine . . .

Did I love her?

Who was she?

"Let's talk. Let's go for a walk. I'd like to call your ex so that I can interview her about you. You would understand, right?"

"Okay, baby. But allow me to kiss you first. Then we'll talk, or something. Just calling my ex like that . . . Is that what you always ask someone you're dating? We're dating, right? What's our status?"

"Yes. We're dating. Yes."

People are so imperfect. It's easy to hate me, to date me or hate me, but I do it all the time, hating my self. Self-loathing contains the only breaths of pity and pride left in all the energy I put out there in the world. Otherwise, I'm a good and decent, honest man. The day my thirtieth birthday comes around, I'll probably be stuck again, like I feel now. I'll be broken-hearted again, so I keep all that's already happened within the marked pages that follow.

The jubilee of today, today's celebration. Nothing never really ends. No. It doesn't. That's what the mind is for. It reminds us of all of that.

Georgie was not as loving as he thought to the woman in his mind. He was not all-good, all-loving. He couldn't be all-knowing. She didn't think he was anything of any good, at all. At least he thinks she thought this way, probably because I was, somehow, thinking something, too.

Ah, what to make of the facts. Philosophy will always rule over the facts.

There was no end between us. There were no final comments, no good-byes, and no point in time when we would have our final falling-out, like a fight or a beating or a baby. She was indifferent toward Georgie, toward me. That was the bitterest pill for me to swallow. She was straight out of an Elvis Costello song, "Shoes Without Heels."

No divorce. No meltdown. No blue balls. No black eye, just heartache, the obsession and corruption of Georgie's integrity. Love beyond his dignity.

She hung over us like a black cloud. She let herself linger there with her powers. She had such luxurious powers over our senses. This whole time, I rummage through my scrapbook and things. Georgie kicks back and thinks of all the shredded porn.

It's been a year I've lived here and a year she lived next door, but the calendar pages have ceased to stop flipping. The days go on, and so do we. It's a part of us, the times, the time, the hours. The awkward seconds of waiting for a new thought to come through. These thoughts become us. We become our own little voices. We dare to extend our true selves. We're all too sick and dishonest to consider omitting what we're really like. We must edit certain things that might otherwise seep out by means of the English language. At least I do. At least I should be considering such an act, the act of shutting Georgie's mouth. Georgie pretends to think. His stream of thoughts make their way back to me. They envelop all that I am. Thoughts of love follow. Feelings and behaviors come after that. Georgie listens in. Can you hear it?

Georgie's been in my head and on my mind since the beginning. But now it's time for him to go. What has already happened should, in sentiment, regain the place it might have lost in real life. We look upon has happened with the eyes of a vulture, glancing for a moment upon the domination of our thoughts and feelings by another soul shattered, a little like the rest of us. We are those who we call us. We are they. We try to make sense of things and move on. The best way we know how.

I'm moving somewhere a little different, someplace new. I'm changing my surroundings.

Georgie, I love you, don't leave.

26. DIALOGUE WITH SELF

-Georgie, Georgie, Georgie . . . When did you figure out that you didn't matter?

That I didn't matter? As soon as I realized that if you only live once, you only die once.

-There's a difference?

Yes. To live life to the fullest is to appreciate life, to have babies, babes, to trust others and to love, to work hard and play hard, to take advantage.

-And you don't believe in all that?

Well, you know that saying, "Life's a bitch and then you die?"

-But there are a lot of good things in life. Good, sweet. A lot of sweetness to suck out of it.

Of course, and you have to take advantage of those times and make them happen, create those scenarios.

-Yes.

But what about Love? The pornographic puzzle? How might I find Love? At the bar? No. At work? No. I don't work. Don't need to. Don't want to. Want to find Love.

-Maybe you should work.

What?

-Work, maybe you should.

And be judged. Paid, paid like shit? Treated like a baby treats a diaper?

-The getting paid part shouldn't mean a thing to you. You've already got a lot of money.

No friends.

-Meet them at work.

Work?

-Do charity work.

Help others? I'm so selfish. And nobody's been helping me.

-Really?

I've only paid for help, paid for friends, hookers, paid for everything. My means is money. I kind of want my life to just end sometimes, now, for once, sometime soon. Sick. Sick. Sick. I mean, I'm just holding out to see if things will get any better on their own.

-Why don't you just get out of your self for once?

But my self isn't even taken care of right. How can I leave my self all by himself?

-Faith?

Fuck faith. Faith that my shit will be smelly? It's always going to be shitty. I mean smelly, stinky.

-Why must you bring up excrement, Georgie?

Because that's what I think of myself. I think it's funny and unavoidable. Ugly women turn me on.

-Good one, Georgie.

They're my possibilities.

-What are your probabilities?

Again, invisibleness, despair, morbid melancholy, mystical terror, eighteenth-century angst. That dull, somber depression you read about in Russian. Moods. Mood swings and the possibility for anything to happen.

-But probably?

Not.

-Interesting. But what if you could change things?

Believe me, I can't.

-You can't change them to your liking?

Right. I've been trying that since the start of things. Things. Me. Since the start of me.

-Change your self? Change the things around you, if you can. Like the serenity prayer. Remember not to think too much, too hard. Don't be too hard on your self. Don't be hard on Georgie. You need him. Respect your thoughts. Got it? Good.

Don't worry. Others are hard on me anyway.

-That's only the way you perceive it.

But that's why I don't matter. Clutter. It makes me sadder. See, my thoughts don't matter.

-Have you ever been butt-fucked? Wholesomely used?

No.

-Honestly?

Yes.

-Is your mind racing and wandering now?

Yes.

156

-Do you feel alone and invisible now?

Yes.

-Must be my fault. But why do you think I care to ask? About you?

Because you are me.

-But you're not thinking my thoughts. I'm thinking yours. My dialogue is mine. It's independent of you. So I don't need to worry about editing my thoughts and things.

The things in my head are nothing notably unusual or of any vital importance. Are they? Not?

-They're unique to you. When you think to yourself, for example, like now. But I see what you're saying. Being noticed and recognized is important. Even personal achievement without others' knowledge of it is pretty worthless.

Unless you're invisible and alone.

-Loneliness need not bring despair. You're smiling so often in all those old photos of you. Whether you're alone or with other people. And the idea of you in those photos is an independent issue. A cause with and without a reason. And with a reason, all the same. Sort of existential.

They're images of you. Like the images in your imagination. So enjoy them. Smile. Laugh at them. At you. For Lord's sake.

-Yes. I know. Generally speaking. I should look for my self-worth and not look against it. Must be there anyway.

If you can imagine so.

-And I can. Besides, your life used to be full. But, now and as time goes on, I can sense you're hurt easily.

Isn't that called "hopeless Romanticism"? My mind's starting to scatter. I'm sorry. I don't drink anymore. I only smoke. Everything's becoming clichéd. My life. Me as a metaphor. My past, what matters most, is disappearing these days! It's depressing, no?

-Calm down. Calm down. Georgie, I'm curious. What do you want?

To be able to spend and create more of my supposed money and affluence. I'm not sure what I have. To have motivation enough to connect with another woman on a level of love and sex. That's what's most important to me. I've never been in love.

Reciprocated love. I've been addicted, addicted to the lie, that's all.

-Do you love your self?

Hell yes and hell no. Depending on my mood and who I'm with and what's going on around me.

-What about right now?

Now's not important. Only the past is, like I said.

-What if now is important and the future is, too? The two of them. Then what?

Overall, no. Because I don't know.

-If you could choose?

Yes.

-Why?

For the others.

-So, it's not all selfish then.

It is. For the others, for me.

-You sound so ridiculous.

No. Brilliant!

-So, you like that about yourself, that you sound brilliant. That you are brilliant.

I like that I don't have to conform to public knowledge or even leave my house to figure out most of the Big Puzzle. It makes me different. I do, however, hate being a philosopher. The answer is so simple. That it continues on in question and new answers are formed. Theories. The answer is that there's no end to ideas. Our imagination is somehow infinite.

-So, Love. So your lover, the next one coming, she must be different, but like you.

No. She must like me. If she ever comes. Cums.

-And love you.

I will love her. I guarantee it.

-Are you having more external thoughts of excrement now?

You got it!

-Focus.

No!

-Does that bother you?

No. But I wish it did. It's a part of my condition.

-Okay.

Okay? No, that's not okay.

-Right. Your thoughts are not the Word of God, like you wrote once.

Right. And I got that from somewhere anyway. Nothing original there.

-Original? Billions of people have existed and not existed already. Of course there are no more original thoughts left. Human imagination has been experienced in all its fullness. For a while. It will continue that way, too. It's impossible to articulate all the thoughts one thinks. Some of them you need to keep to yourself. Especially when the mind's speeding.

But, all in all, I just can't figure myself out. There's this woman . . .

-Try to figure somebody else out then. There's too much else to worry about.

How am I supposed to fit more figuring out in my life?

-I think you're scared.

Of course I am.

-Because you don't know.

It's got to be better than this. This life.

-Well, why don't you just wait until your next mood swing?[45]

Hey, come back. Come back. That sucks. We're not finished. You're abandoning me. I'm abandoning me.[46]

---

[45] . . . This alter ego exits.

[46] . . . This alter ego falls asleep, wishing fatal dreams of giving up.

27. FAMILY REUNION

Some minor details: Georgie used to wear huge, round, horn-rimmed glasses until he lost them. He ended up getting a pair of Lennon specs afterwards. He grew a goatee and his hair long around that time. He cut the crap by the time his Perplexity intruded on his little lack of a life.

He had a lot going for him. He still tries to stand out. In fact, he's wearing a pink and aqua-blue button-down shirt today. But then again, Georgie hasn't left the house yet to show it off, or let the ladies think he's lovely; all this he thinks while he could be whistling some silly tune down the street, possibly meeting up with somebody new, a stranger, while being "out there."

He looks in the mirror. The sides of his basic designer blouse are drenched with armpit sweat. He examines himself. He gets manicures and pedicures. He curls his hair and uses a blow dryer. He waxes his eyebrows. He's turning into such a girl. Maybe it's a DNA thing.

They say some boys develop into men even when they've got two X chromosomes, like a girl. Maybe he had a cord transfusion with the blood of a girl as an infant. Maybe that's why he's so sick and feels so strange, maybe not.

After all, he's straight and sober. His history is straight, straightforward.

The summer sun screams with pure energy. Georgie's nervous tics pop to some simple song skipping in his head. He dances to it with complexity. He jerks his head. He tells people he can't help it, that he's sorry.

He'll be hooking up with the extended family for a little reunion back in the Hamptons. (Well, it's in a smaller, poorer section near the Hamptons where the staff members of the glitzy estates live, but it's the same thing.)

Part of him still lives in the cult of luxury, but he's still very much alone. (Kindly refrain from any jealousy if you're the jealous type. You can trade your life in by the end. It's just might take a while.)

P.S. Don't trade it. Believe me.

Before the holiday, Georgie had been getting some long-awaited phone calls from a couple of people who would be attending the reunion: cousins, etc. who were checking in ahead of time. The pre-reunion, if you will. Everyone was checking to see what they were up against in the family wars. Who had disappeared, who died? Knowing as much as possible about the others, all beforehand, was of vital importance.

After the party, the individual attendees could gossip about what they actually saw in the others who were there. Georgie had gained some weight since the last family reunion, for instance. Many people told him he "looked different," indirectly mentioning what they really noticed, that his looks had changed for the worse, his appearance, his fat ass and inappropriate love handles. Georgie responds to these check-in phone calls, the few of them that come through, with an air of being grounded. He tries to ask the interrogators about their shitty little days.

They all seemed to have some kind of life, things going on, events and circumstances, trials and trivia all for some main purpose, all to move everything else along with the tide, actual connections with real people, collaborative connections, and positive directions.

Georgie had a plan to tell them nonchalantly that he's had some things in his life, some things he was working on, some promising endeavors, things in the works. He was keeping busy with work and stuff.

But by the time he got the cue, Georgie would end up kicking himself in the face, describing in detail all of his newfound weaknesses, all the new additions since he and whoever had last spoken. He would end up telling them the truth, the way he saw things, from down there, in his head.

He believed that someone out of the blue might someday actually listen to him with understanding and make him happy. Inside, there were no smiles. Without words, he was desperately begging someone from the inside to turn on some switch in the boardroom that would turn the tables around. He wanted to feel new and positive things, good things that would last for the better. But that switch had never even been there to begin with.

The relatives would finish their interrogations and end up not calling Georgie back for another year, even when Georgie himself would make the attempt to connect in the time between. Those calls were neither taken nor returned. That's why the weekend of Labor Day was continually a dismal time, every year.

Georgie, still sitting down, lights a fresh cigarette. He thinks about when and where he lost that edge he used to have, when he was on top of his game, when he was a winner.

He would dance and play with new ideas and thoughts. He used to be able to see the beauty in things for example. But his gifted creativity, his selfish back-tickling, these ideals he had lost touch with. There was only the nostalgia left from those more innocent times.

His self was so attractive to him. It was a safety zone. It was a lie. Lies are usually very attractive. Georgie's blue balls hurt like a small weight was sitting on the scrotum. It was a constant pain. The anxiety he was putting up with manifested itself on the skin. He would get this herpes-like fever blister mess on the corners of his mouth and on his lips; his genitals were another story, and the strong heat outside was no help.

Georgie hated the heat. He would always have the A/C on high, even in the car when the windows were open. He even had a unit installed in his master bathroom that would blow out cold air. Georgie's bedroom had two of them. His bedroom was small.

He was going to bed for the night around three in the morning these days. He lit his last smoke for the night and dwelled on the upcoming family event, making a big deal out of nothing. Then he got a second wind.[47]

He'd probably make a couple of jokes about turning gay or something to cover up all his embarrassment and fear. I know it's all good anyway, they'll think. I still like him. So what if he's without a woman.[48]

There's no such thing as true uniqueness, or something like that.[49]

---

[47] I'll be the only one there without a date.

[48] But every year? Hell, I'm not any different from the others. It's everyone else who's different.

[49] Georgie, shut up!

The events of the day started to replay in Georgie's head. They would end up becoming part of the dreams he would have afterwards, but the nightmares would have a more profound effect on him. He hated to suffocate in fires and drown in two inches of water or burn in the house while the firemen just watched and let it all happen.[50]

---

[50] I should have asked out the bagger at the supermarket, that Ashley chick. Damn her.

28. HALLOWEEN

Georgie's brain starts to process thought.

Images are formed.

"Is happiness what you're really striving for?"

"Do you know what you want?"

"The ultimate goal is freedom."

"The Desert Island Disco."

"Activities and relationships to pick and choose from."

"Are you in love?"

"Do you know what you need?"

"What makes you feel good?"

"Do you smile sometimes because it's ethical?"

"Clubs and categories you loathe preoccupy your thinking. Do they take up your daily life?"

"You're a lifetime member of society. What about your lifetime membership to the gym?"

"You have a gift. You owe it to the world. You owe it to yourself to share your talent."

Georgie hears people telling him this.

"Everything seems so dramatic."

"You're more than stressed out. You don't have depression. You feel worse than shit. It's only the symptoms of anxiety. It's in your head."

"You think you have too many memories and consider them symptoms of despair. Everything your senses collect is buried in the depths of nostalgia."

"Your life seems like an insipid gathering of time in heaps."

"Others tell you you're fine. You think they're fucking with you."

"You always knew you were different. So did everyone else."

"You take medication. You used to call it medicine. Your meds may need adjustment. It's okay now to tell others what you're on."

"You reveal yourself in déjà vu so that it ends abruptly."

"You have a few good friends. Most good people do. All of them fail to be there for you when you need them most. They created who you are, in all your fullness."

"They called you an old soul. You consider being brand new."

"You're constantly trying to change your life. You spend most of the time only talking about the changes you want to make."

"You fail to make a full commitment and follow through one hundred percent."

"Conform to a little popularity. Read the latest bestseller. Make sure it's a self-help book. Do the exercises they suggest. Create your day. It's that simple."

"You analyze everything. You should be dating somebody else."

"You give and take too much. Try moderation."

"Complain about big corporations and the government. Continue to pay them out of need."

"You leave your past behind. It starts creeping back already."

"You think you live in a fairy tale."

"You think life is clichéd."

"You don't really think you'll ever die."

"You might start thinking about everything soon, something concrete, something hard, something personal. I'm not talking about you."

29. FIRST DATE WITH PERPLEXITY

I imagine what it was like, our first date. It's foggy outside and I'm real anxious, until Claudia solidifies and she finally exists. I'm hungry. I'm thirsty. *Where and when does this date take place?* I ask myself. I hear Georgie answering all my questions in my head.

"Don't look at her."

"Tell her of your flaws, your fears, and your needs."

"Make sure she's aware of your high-maintenance personality."

"Shhhh! Quiet!" I say, until Georgie does the date for me. He always gets what I want.

Georgie and Claudia are at the fusion restaurant.

A sushi dinner for two, table for four.

Their first public date would begin with a light knock at her front door.

"Tap-tap." *Do we hallucinate noise?* I ask myself and knock again, twice.

It was all the noise Georgie had the balls to make.

No doorbell.

"Tap-tap." Again, no loud noises. Besides, the door was already open a crack.

He stepped back a bit, hesitating for an answer.

"Come!" he heard.

Claudia sounded like an aristocrat answering a peasant's wish to enter in some old period piece film.

"Let's go," Georgie said, so impolitely.

She pretended she was surprised to see him.

"Princess!"

"Just kidding."

They walked together up their street to the commercial district where all the shops and restaurants were. Georgie held her left hand. He was on her left side so he could grasp her with his right hand. But Snicker Doodle wanted Georgie on the other side.

"I was battered over the head with a wine bottle from that side," she revealed, "and I still have this fear . . . Could we just switch sides?"

"Okay, baby."

Georgie didn't know if she was pulling his chain or not. But he did feel a strong desire to see her naked at that point. He required proof that her history with other men ended through his fault and not hers.

Georgie needed to see the damage done—any and all scars.

He could intuitively sense she was a liar. But he didn't know what she lied about. Maybe she was a chick with a dick, a witch, a bitch. A prick-tease with a disease. He couldn't say for sure.

Would he end up lying to her, too?

"I have schizophrenia," he declared.

His Perplexity didn't mind.

Georgie was told she was a social worker.

"My mind plays tricks on me," Georgie threw out.

"It does? So does mine."

The score was even.

The new couple ate their dinner then headed back to Snicker Doodle's little sanctuary down the street. On the way back, Georgie recalled her offer to pay half of the supper bill, but Georgie wouldn't hear of that. The thought crossed his mind that he should have let her pay the whole thing, especially having looked back on it by the time it was it was too late.

Before their goodnights, Georgie stood with her by the front door to her place.

"I don't want—I don't want to fuck you, Georgie. Just so you know . . . I don't want to fuck you," said Claudia.

"May I touch your breasts?"

"No, not yet. Thanks for asking, though. Thanks, Georgie."

30. FROM THE INSIDE

Georgie jerks off then writes another shitty poem. The Nervous Narcissist listens in. His teeth sparkle as he hears his alter ego speak to him. I am alone. But not bored. It's over now. We're done and through. These things we used to do.

#

Claudia looked Georgie in the eyes, breathing that same sick-dizzy, sad-puppy, bulldozing, THIS IS THE END look you'd expect just before a breakup. Georgie wished she could see for herself how pathetically she was coming off. If she only knew how unattractive her true California girlishness reflected off her face; it was so clichéd, so stereotypical. Georgie had a burning urge to slap that shit hard. But what Snicker Doodle wanted was unclear. Even at age forty. She was still fucking around with several people at the same time. These relationships were sexual.

Georgie wondered if she was ever miserable. He's pissed off thinking she has never been burned herself. He quit smoking again. He wants to light up. He will later, one more cigarette later, somewhere, sometime, he bites his teeth.

"Was Claudia miserable even if just slightly, ever?"

His Perplexity might eventually get with a seventy-year-old wrinkled cockroach she'd end up butchering in the sac, some Newport Beach land developer with a terminal heartbeat and lots of money. He'd end up married to the bitch-love, undercover, a little discreetly. He'd croak in bed, beside her, long before her.

Get the gun, Georgie.

The old man might leave Snicker Doodle with next to nothing except a free ticket to the funeral. This won't happen. Her luck's too good. Georgie feels like a stalker. He is. He's a fucking mess, mentally tortured.

#

Diary, Journal, Self, Whomever, Whatever, maybe Dr. C:

Look, I cannot tolerate the current symptoms I'm experiencing, in-and-out. It's taking me a long while to even get anything down here, but for my life, I put out the best effort I could ever make.

My head is a constant firecracker, my tongue curls up and wisps out through my puckering lips, my mouth contorted, extending the skin under my mustache and lower beard areas. My head snaps rapidly and with extreme force, all on its own and with every incoming thought or fragment of one, any bit of self-awareness, the head will jerk to a singular, asymmetrical beat, but usually, un-rhythmically to a POUND after POUND, POUND-POUND, with different intensities. The thoughts want to escape.

All I can still think about are my stories, my work. I don't want down-time, free-time, Georgie Time. My work is required. Period.

I must keep my voice low. Others, from all around, hear me. They are suspicious, and they almost spy on me. Earlier, cars were beeping at me; people on the streets and in the parking lots were snickering in those same whispers I hear at night, about me. They look away before I can get a look at who they are. They're real, and it's tempting to know who they are, especially if they've got a cell phone on them or are with another person. They might want to call the cops, for my suspiciousness. Cars back off to a distance when behind me or at my side at a red light. Sometimes the passengers cover their faces as if what they're saying is secret. When the traffic moves faster, other cars held their horns down at me twice, so I thought I had run someone off the road. I look back and it has stopped. People yell, but this is not typical. Police sirens and helicopter noise come and go, when I shift into second or third gear. The energy's high, and these noises dissipate no sooner than they had started. Maybe two seconds in duration. Some of the whispers came back while I made it to my first destination. Dropping off my landlord's check in Seal Beach is a fifteen-minute drive. The ladies from the hair salon were snickering about me. I heard "He's the one" come from one of their mouths, quietly. Then they walked back inside. I wrote out my note to the landlord and kept my cool.

My head snapped again. I couldn't focus on the red lights, but I handled it better today than yesterday. I didn't sit through a few cycles of them. While driving back, I could barely drive well, with my head snapping and eyes rolling, my hands coming off the steering wheel and into a finger-stretching, waving-like gesture. The music was not helping, even back home.

I've been so confused, I forget how to turn on my video camera, make coffee, or find keys (it took me three hours this morning to find my car keys). This medication I took an hour ago is making me feel internally dizzy. My head tics are still present. I feel a little high. I could definitely not drive now or go outside, open any windows or blinds; I must choose which phone calls to take, if any—I might soon be craving the hallucinations that usually come in higher doses of whatever-it's-called. I miss them.

It's a half-hour later. I'm fucking stoned on this shit. I need help, an aide, a live-in, something. I cannot function as a person currently. I'm really scared, but the paranoia for now, I can't believe it, is either different or less. I don't want anybody (neighbors, etc.) to see me. What I'm feeling must definitely show in my outer being. I'm not sure how. I'd be scared to know. The doctor will call me soon. I'm not sure if I'm explaining these symptoms right. I get so utterly confused. I'm losing my mind. I can't think of any treatment that would help. Is this terminal? Will this tend to worsen? What is it, really? I need to make my mark somehow on the world. My friends can't show up for me. I haven't dared tell them of my misery, up and down.

#

Let's try even harder. *I'm as okay as people say I am. I trudge along. I dictate my own misery. But, by the name of God, there's a reason for this drudgery. I'm ready to start the day, again. I woke up on my own again, before my seven-hour alarm. Such a matter has grown into a sort of repetitive routine. Like the same nightmares I experienced again, last night, or rather, this morning.*

My neck and throat's manifestations of Tourette's continue to worsen. I'm making a valid attempt at writing as much as I can bear, in the hope that some of these night terrors and the morbid confusion of the day will dissipate.

Yesterday was horrendous. The night before, Georgie put on a dream patch, one of those patches fuelled with nicotine. He's armed with one every night during sleep so he can dream, vivid and lucid. More lucid when he's got the classical radio station on, or even the television, something to actually present the dream images and scenarios to him.

The night before last, he dreamt his best friend Bobby Banks was being wed to a pop star. The angst that the dream images caused was uncomfortable, and Georgie's imagination became wounded afterwards. He knew his best friend Bobby Banks was a faithful man—thus, the angst. I have become a faithful man, in my recovery. Yet, I feel distanced, almost abandoned from my best friend at the same time.

Claudia is promiscuous and lie-worthy. She represents the nonchalant confusion, not of my heart, but of my perception. Others don't see things the same way. This morning's dreamscape involved the same "I'm suffocating ..." I'm not able to make my mark on the world. I can't leave my neighbor, and I'm trying to grow stronger with this unbearable pressure of something so tiny. A woman who is just as bisexually needy as a straight man needs pussy. Claudia couldn't kiss me when I stopped by to give her the greeting cards for her new apartment. Sara was nearby.

"No. No. We can't kiss here. It's inappropriate," Claudia said. That's why I left her before. That's why I'm addicted to this woman. I have nowhere else to go. How might I escape her but rely on the finding of other love? Am I really a damaged person?

I want to say, "You fucking lush, dyke. You, who fucks with my mind, in my nightmares, I want to kill myself because you exist. I hate myself because of you. Huh? Would other guys go for this? How can that be? Are they now? It's been over a year, you waste. No, I don't love you."

172

She answers, "You just make me want to ask you to sleep with me again and again."

I vomited on her face and on her chest, and she said the same thing about sleeping with her because of the mess I was.

"Get a life," she echoed, "get a life, Georgie-boo, I'll see you again soon."

What lies deep in her past? I'll never know. This character in my experience . . . What a bitter sharp stinging pinch. It hurts. It makes me tic. I pucker my lips and "click." I need out, but I still feel I need to make my mark first. This is most important to me—discovering myself so that I can manifest the outcome artistically. Every day, I collect the moments of time and shove them inside until I'm about to burst. But I don't. There is, perhaps, a good reason for this. I could be a very new soul, so to speak. I'm more depressed than Claudia has a shit day.

"I'm having a shit day," she'd confess every Wednesday for reasons I'll never know about.

Her internal turmoil doesn't manifest itself outside. So, again, I've felt this feeling some other time in my life, too, déjà vu again.

But I'm jealous that she can balance such a fucking crazy life so nonchalantly. How can I be a better person? I'm unable to do this, but it's exactly what I crave in my attempts at writing. So perhaps I am learning, the hard way again. I need this shitty relationship as a part of my plan. I'm getting closer to finding it the more I write, even think, even cry, when I drain myself through such outlets like writing, thinking, letting the thoughts seep out a little, or emotionally, when I cry in the shower, with music, alone, softly, with fear. I hone in, getting closer to the truth about me. To know myself, not in its pretentiousness, but genuinely, I will be able to have a relationship with the world, with the social and familial climates I'm now so uncomfortable with. My mark is somewhere in there. Then, all the rest can fall into their own places, as they lie within the subtle moments that breed happiness on a local platform. I really feel this. It's all, really, a matter of time and sticking with it, never giving up, in my imagination.

I puff away on my cigarette. I find out I'm mad. I realize what it takes to be a king, more than I know. What tools I might need. It gets a little clearer—the more I feed the solitude with things that I know. I'm so limited by what I used to use as an excuse, my medical maladies, whether in-born, genetic, or from abuse, neglect, the environment, and life. I want to leave this world and come back with something remote and profound. I want to change universal thought. I've got to keep in constant contact with the doctor today. I cancelled the trip to San Francisco. I'm as stressed out as I was as a teenager.

Let me lose my mind and get over this. Someone, God, please help me. Don't let me go yet. I still take it all too seriously. I know of no other way.

31. THE SLOW FADE-OUT

MON JUNE 27 10:29 PM.

"Hey Georgie. It's about 10:30. Anyway. I'm just going to stop working and go to bed. I don't even know when you called me. Anyway. Fiscal year ends. You know. Of course. This week. So there's a big push to get reports in. And charts and paperwork and audits and everything. Done. So. Anyway. So. That's where I'm kind of focusing. And then after Friday. Well that should be nice. I should have a break. Anyway. I hope things are good with you. And that's it. I'll catch up with you later. Hopefully, you're having beautiful dreams right now. And. I guess good morning as well. Probably when you'll receive this. Mmm. Bye."

#

Sleep deprivation: You just want the next day to come soon having had a full night's rest. A new beginning is needed. I need a short story. What I really need is a high-concept, great-story piece. A script to film that would get a good soundtrack. The script, a page-turner, the film, a tear-jerker, the audience, truly involved. What could this story be? I need to find this story. Is it a mix of what I've got now or a brand-new idea—using what I've learned from what I've got now? Could I write it fast? Could I pound it out, like putty? What are the themes? In what order? Love. Buddies. Friendship. Obsession. Moving on. Identity. Adventures in setting. At least three. Death. Loneliness. Despair. Philosophy. Intelligence. Generation X. Affluence. The Honda Generation.

32. END OF NOVEMBER

I wanted to give her the finger. Shoot her a real big FUCK YOU, but what about me? I kept planning what I was going to do the next time I'd see her next door. Maybe I'd get a good-bye. For the past week, she'd been parking her car right near my back door. Right near the garage, near the office at home, near the kitchen. The doors I frequently use to get from here to there, dosing up on caffeine and sugar, my mind screaming.

You're still in love with her. You're still in love.

Where was Georgie when I needed him the most? She was alone, and I ran and fell into her arms. Hopelessly, pathetically, profoundly in one long, over-expired love epic. The epic love affair of the century rests in my heart, my butchered, tormented, tortured, wrecked, strong and very weak and tired heart, its thumping beats overlapping in a sound prairie, a thunderstorm of bolts crashing, scissors chopping, teeth clenching recklessly. Letting havoc rip out of my soul, giving in to all the temptation Georgie could ever bear to stand for the rest of his life.

Yesterday . . .

Today started as fucked up as it ended. Good. It was good. This whole time, I'd been trying to understand myself and to be understood by others. I was a closet pervert. Now I'm a public pervert. So is Georgie. And he can still function in a normal daily living scenario, as normal as things will get, at least for now. I need to exercise my mind. Need to get some more things out. Have sex with my mind until my mind has an orgasm and splashes. All its sweet love was once stored inside. I fucked it. Ah. It had little to do with this morning or tonight, today. It started last night. It started a few weeks ago. It started when Georgie had been trying to rid his Perplexity from his head and have sexual intercourse with somebody else so that she would no longer be THE LAST ONE. Georgie lights a cigarette and starts puffing. He's on his tenth shot of espresso today and just starting to get down to the nitty-gritty. His phone's been ringing off the hook all day.

33. NARCISSIST

Let me lose my mind. Fuck it. I'm going out for a walk on the beach. The beach is a block away. The voices in my head are raging. They're calling me a winner.

I've already done my damage in this lifetime and paid for it. I'm okay. It's the others I'm concerned about. It's me. It's all the chaos. I remember breaking up with her twice, that little princess, that unthinkable seductress, *my Perplexity.*

I've got to vent a little. I just learned what June Gloom meant last week, from hearing Claudia talk about it. I've lived out here for five years. Is it even a West Coast term?

What is it that I even want? I have no idea how far I'm going to walk. Am I after happiness? The city built this pathway on the beach to encourage exercising. That's nice. The rain fell last night without a pause. It came down to a slight drizzle this morning. I look at my watch. I wait for time to pass. I wonder how far I'm going. This walking makes me feel good. What else does? Is that important to me? I think I'm pretty giving, but there's a narcissist inside me at the same time. I wonder if that's common. Hell, in humans, anything's common. God, I'm getting blisters already. I wish I didn't smoke. Let me get my mind off this.

I collapse on the beach and close my eyes. If I'm ever be able to get to the point, I'll have to keep going over it and over it, again and again, until perfection.

This is where I'm stuck, enough generalities.

Claudia, everyone, Claudia, Claudia, what's the next big thing? Who will be the next big death? What about the next big technology, or the next big fad, or the next killer drug?

I suck down another cigarette. I can't smoke in my office. This tiny little aristocratic shithole office I often call my Little Think Tank Room. I've implied I was frustrated. So what?

I'm dying. I've only got fifteen more days to live the way I see it. I'd say it's somewhere between the fifteenth of December and the twenty-fifth, this year. I won't see the next year when it comes, if it comes. I won't leave my twenties. I won't see, hear, taste, smell, or touch again, I won't remember, or experience anything else. I will no longer exist. I have to write all this stuff down before it's too late. I don't know why I've waited. I didn't know any better.

It has to be about me now, doesn't it? I can feel it. I can feel the nausea, phlegm-coughing, anxiety, paranoia, loneliness, bitterness, and nostalgia. I start to laugh hysterically at my own demise. It lasts for an hour, a fraction of my life. I knew I'd be an early death, since I was a kid, in fact.

Now I'm not sure if my life was worth it, or if my death will be meaningful.

34. THE ORANGE BUTTON

I checked into another hotel. I should have signed up for points when I first started staying here. Would it be another hassle, another scam? I can't stand all the junk mail that comes with any membership. I get so confused with all the sign-up forms. Maybe I'll sign up later. I'll ask at the front desk before I leave. The front desk clerk knows me and my situation. I come and I go, often. My stays lack any consistency. But who cares? I needed to get away again. I needed change. But the same things still haunt me.

I'm addicted to change, even coming back to something if it means switching gears. I'm in the same room I had before. I'm all too familiar with that little orange button on the remote that says ORDER in thin black letters. I remove the top bedspread. I put toilet paper on the porcelain tank and try not to make the tanning lotion look like it's been used at all. I take down a washcloth and start fantasizing. That's why I'm back here.

Everything's at my disposal.

I find myself drawing naked pictures for hours, staying up at night, forcing myself to the edge of insomnia, half-awake, half-baked, but I'm clean. I lost the consistency, charm, and nonchalance I once had. I perfected it, and it shattered right before me. I was in my mid-twenties, somewhere. I make a small effort to regain a sense of self-discipline. It's tough to get back into the swing of things. All my routines have shut down.

Can all the paradoxes in life be worked out through calculus? Why didn't I get that far in school? Did I grow up too fast, too spoiled? Is this what being an adult is like for others?

I need a home, a home base, a starting point, a life lesson.

I write in haste so as to come to some conclusion about my actual position in this life. I'm worried and paranoid. I don't want to be filmed, but there are spy cams everywhere. I can see my funeral from above, like in a dream, with some friends who might attend. I'm outside myself, but in self. There's a lot of '80s music, a dance, and Bach's Toccata and Fugue in D Minor. I show up on a video screen and tell everybody how much it hurts to die. I send them my greetings and let them know I am watching them from the dead side. I prepared for this, sort of. People put things in my coffin, a cell phone, letters, pornography, and paraphernalia. Then they raid my house. They take keepsakes to remember me by. Afterwards, they inquire what really happened to me. I die without a will because I had too much other work. This leaves the people with a lot of angst and feelings of betrayal. It's an open coffin, and my eyes are open. The paramedics caught me in the nude and didn't leave me a tip. My heart was bleeding. I said no pictures.

Everyone in this building will promptly forget the life and times of me and whereupon I will live in the further hearts of others who might or might not have showed up. They will keep me immortal. Who cares? My consciousness is gone. I left all my worries. I'm dwelling in some other dimension, maybe even the fifth. I like the fifth. It welcomes me back whenever I revisit. I hadn't been back in a while, ever since the incident at the bank. Two guardian angels comfort me, and I walk around the Earth like everyone else. I'm dead. I question whether I ever existed until now. All my memories are restarted.

I'm rambling again. The doctor just listens. I don't feel anything. I can't seem to shut my mouth. I still can't find my house keys. I don't like this idea of a hide-a-key business. I was already robbed once. It took a while to recover. My house is a mess anyway. That's why I try to get away. Fast. Here at the hotel. Everything is at my fingertips. Everything is fast. Just like the times. Love though, love can't always be rushed. I've seen examples of fast things destroy people and put them in debt. It's a modern concept.

I'm thankful I've got some money and a rich family. There's nothing like saving a relationship with your parents. What about all this saved time?

35. BROKEN-HEARTED JUBILEE

Enough was enough.

Enough coffee and cigarettes, drugs, sugar, weight gain, hard liquor and beer, sex and self. Habits and addictions. Fears and phobias. Money and resentment.

Thinking little about the consequences first, I took a drive up to Fat Anne's palatial tent up in Palos Verdes to say, "Listen, baby, I'm through. I'm finished." Fat Anne was not Anne the bartender from way back whenever in my old drinking days in Manhattan. Fat Anne was my good friend. Quirky little alternative pagan—that little starlet song-bird she was.

I wanted to tell her face-to-face since she knew me better than I knew myself, having been diagnosed with something, anything, a little in-between diseases like I was, "otherwise not specified" stuff . . . and she showed the most compassion and sympathy of anyone I knew at the time.

Fat Anne was a woman, confident in her obesity, assertive and feministic, neo- fashion slut, Lane Bryant, eBay bidder whom I met at the local Tourette's support group. She was a lesbian, and her tics were top-notch, a better finger stretch than my retarded one and a "head-banger blast" better than my "Beethoven's mad head-shaker." We shared a common mind of madness and were both attacked by a constant flow of imps. Fat Anne was to disappoint me as well, in the long run.

As I was leaving her pad, she looked at me darkly and said, "Georgie, you know what? You're selfish, more than you realize, and I don't want to be your friend anymore. Anyway, thanks for stopping by, it saved me from writing you an e-mail."

Amber Sirkus called on my way back home. I refused to take her call so she left a voice message. "Did you get the bad news from Anne yet? Call me back. You never call me. Bye."

Fat Anne was my best friend. A temporary friend from whom I would take all that I could until the bridge between us would be broken. I gave her things, too, like my heart, like rent money, but all sappiness aside, I'll be better off sticking with acknowledging the worst in me.

I dreamt last night that I was at a benefit dinner with four women with whom I was sexually involved. This other Princess, a mysterious recurring dream character, known to me only as Lisette, approached me and said, "Could you sleep with me? Or do you want to stay here with them?" The others in the ballroom looked at me, looking around at the others at my table as they smoked their cigarettes and sipped sake. I replied to Lisette, with such disdain, "Yeah, I'd like to stay with them." It was like Lisette symbolized who I represented in Claudia's real life, always checking to see if Claudia would fuck me, just one more time, and again after that, since she couldn't love me. What an ass of me. I can't stand myself.

At home, my bed was broken from all who had been with me there. It wasn't Claudia's fault.

I start to cry, the little angst-ridden baby inside me. Crying is the best therapy.

Silly me, always trying to find a new love that will last.

I just woke up, suffering from an excess of emotion and exaggerated sensitivity to everything that's going wrong around here. In my mind, in my fat, bloated stomach. My sense of self and sick, desperate attraction to all that's taboo and sexual define me. My expectations are quite inflated. I'm self-indulgent. What do I need? To overcome my selfishness through self-discipline, to know life by knowing, really knowing, myself.

I look to Georgie Gust for that.

I pack up my things and head to the local hotel, craving a room with cold air. The heat, dampness and darkness of a private hell, a secret weariness here at home have me suffocating into a self I can hardly bear any longer. No need to sympathize with me; I feed on this solitude. I revel in it. I know little about anything else. My racing thoughts are tied up in knots. The depression and angst, schizoaffective, mind-losing, self-deprecating, self-induced hell in my head, hallucinations, and hypocrisy leave room for me to become a better man.

These are only thoughts. Not the Word of God or anything, so I don't worry. I light a new cigarette and listen to the neighbors drinking beer outside.

What a smooth intro.

Broke up with Melanie last night. Having burnt that bridge, built for but two weeks of bliss, our passion lasted only that long, until our opinions of each other were cooled down to mere indifference.

On a good note, I got to sleep all day and received no phone calls. It's pathetic. You might as well hate me, but I need this outlet.

Mock me, anger me, and put me to shame.

Until then . . .

36. MODERN MALE YOUTH

Modern day, a landscape of fast service, fast food, fast car, fast computer, fast-paced city, make a fast buck, fast recovery from illness, fast fuck, fast thoughts, fast change, lose weight fast, fast delivery, fast credit, fast college degree, fast clean-up, fast frame (movie), surgery (plastic), buildings and condos, fast calculations and analysis, fast photo, in-and-out jails, growing up fast, fast vision correction, modernization, fast product development, fast payment, meals in a bottle or bar, approval, news, life, death.

Do I need to conform? Can I be *them*? Am I a member of Society? Have I rebelled enough yet? Can this be blamed on my childhood? I should try harder to exist. Life is short. I need to follow through 100%. I need to make commitments. I need to make choices. I wear my shoes without socks. I wear store-brand briefs that are stained. I wake up from reality and have a two-minute meeting with my creator. I'm so cheap that way. I give an hour to my shrink. I pray to be rescued, corrected, as long as it's God's will. But my spirit has stifled naturally. I'm ashamed. I apologize for my existence. I really fucked up.

How come, kiddo?

The times that make me, don't make me a man, so I withdraw from the realities I choose not to accept. All this preparation and control in the mad belief that a little creativity might possibly surface from a subconscious quarter of the film-less armoire up here. The idea is classic. I experience in my own selfish way some information, add a little light for my circuitry to process and rearrange a few letters that combined, and form an original idea. I'll fall in love. I'll lose her, unexpectedly and without any foreseeable outcome. Something will come up. I'll change. I'll have some motivation by the end, a new outlook, a new beginning in the garden, a rebirth of my innocence, a simple realization. I think I know what it is, but I'll tell you later.

I'm going through another phase. Last week, I started on this business of saying "absolutely" to project my agreement. I couldn't stand how that sounds even though I like hearing myself talk. My sister does this "bye-bye" trick at the end of a phone call. I don't know how she keeps it up. Sometimes there's a preamble to it when she's sick of the conversation at hand. She'll go "Mmm, bye-bye," and I want to strangle her for cutting me off like a cold caller. I'm craving change in all that I do and think. The idea of me falling in love for real is always with, simply "my girl," my reason, *my Perplexity*. And I still can't sleep.

I look down at my handmade drawing of a woman stalking me in public and puke. I get up the next afternoon, another day wasted. But I've got some ideas. I might need to lie or exaggerate, but I'm inspired by truth. Actually, I'm kind of joking.

Use your imagination. Rent a movie or something. Try something new. Try gossiping. Let me lose my mind. I've got to vent a little. I'm back on my meds. Anti-psychotics, opiate blockers, schizophrenia, angst, Tourette's, and a virus, the bug that's always "going around." I've got that, too. Anxiety and depression, loneliness, catatonic psychosis, loss of self and delusion, a beer belly.

My mind expands, now letting ideas run loose. I'm the switchboard operator up here, nothing's automatic. Picking and choosing, focusing and letting go, those elements are at stake and I'm worried. I don't want to be a product. I can buy a little happiness, but I don't really want to be happy. In my own miniature world, I know everything immediately around me. All the rest I fear. I can only imagine what I don't already know. That's why I smoke so much.

I hear everything. My peripheral vision captures stuff on the side, buries it in my long-term memory, unless I'm in a lucid dream or I'm creating my own experience by guessing what I should find when I turn around, looking in a mirror, pretending I've only got access to two dimensions.

I used to smoke a lot of rock cocaine and watch movies on a blank white wall. There was no projector. Everything is overwhelming and lost. Everything, everyone, they; it's all the same. We get it. I didn't suppose when I came home with a pet kitten when I bought my first place in New York that she'd tear apart my furniture. Is that existential? Is it Nobel Prize-worthy? Am I getting ahead of myself, me, the dick? Existence precedes essence. Maybe essence also comes before. I wish I knew for sure. But I don't.

The landscape in the background is beautiful. Once again, I sense the living colorful beauty by walking outside; sometimes outside is the mental battlefield, but still halfway in my head. That's where I speak from, most times, I know.

I resent that I blew my trust fund way too early. I yearn for a second chance and want to make it on my own. We'll have to see. How could somebody do that? How could somebody have done that, long ago? Is nature circular, or evolutionary, or static? Question after question causes too many answers, too much bullshit, conspiracy, and relativity. Can you believe that? Who's to blame? The creation of more jobs, minimum wage jobs at fast food places. This absurd, stupid high-as-hell standard of living these days . . . The end of "the job" . . . What might that bring? I've rarely worked at a normal job. I'm waiting for the next big thing.

More fired . . . more fires, more buildings. Has the past burned away? Can it be restored quickly? Let's drink to that. Let's pass out and die. Let's steal.

"Why?"

What would our founding fathers think now? I contemplate deeply. Where would they go? How would they get there? When will information databases come off the ground? Will work be done in the connection of information, or will we just send and receive information through the air. Nice picture. When would some affluence lead us to more freedom? Freedom of choice is freedom of self, freedom of will, ideas, beliefs, and blame. Freedom to sleep . . . sheep . . . sleep . . . (Sleep.) And this recurring theme, this island where I become free, even in my dreams, I get stuck there. Stuck in freedom, all this excess, all this all-or-nothing business.

#

Her Last Words:

"You know what? I just don't have the time to give you. I just don't," Claudia said with such disdain.

—*Claudia, Heidi . . . My Perplexity.*

37. TRANSITION INTO THE DRAMA OF SELF

I took it all in, stuffed it deep inside, real hard. Within a few minutes . . . I headed to the garage, my shadow followed me there.

"Georgie," I said, "Get in the fucking car, you fucking bitch!"

His image started swimming into focus so I could believe he was really there. He was still the same hotshot hallucination made up merely of my own misperceptions. He appeared to be a spitting image of my fat ass and fat head and bad fucking breath. He was just as big of an asshole as I was. Except that he did nothing wrong and I blamed myself for everything. I never learned the proper way to deal with conflict. Once the excitement of any new relationship faded away, any conflict that would naturally follow dragged me into a fear of unknowing where I would simply call that particular relationship quits.

Catching myself in this awareness, aware of the awareness itself that I was about to burn the bridge with myself, through Georgie, I popped on the CD changer in the car, having fired up the German-guzzling ignition, the key-in-the-hole DING-DING followed by Pink Floyd's "Wish You Were Here." I put the speakers on Hi-Fi and strapped up and smoked the rear wheels out of the garage. Georgie and I were silent and stern-eyed, as I ran through the stop sign at the corner.

Can you tell heaven from hell?
Blue skies from pain?

—Pink Floyd

At the first red light, a sudden agonizing realization came to me that every light we would hit would turn red before we hit it, so I stopped the car then and there, shut the engine off, and locked the keys inside. Georgie got out, and I followed. He knew what I was up to better than I did myself. But I took my anger out on Georgie anyway.

"Have you lost it completely?" I forced out with a hint of spit and scat.

Georgie opened the passenger door with ease and slipped back inside the car. He showed me the key he had dangling from his fingertips and started to laugh.

Your heroes for ghosts . . .

—Pink Floyd

I grabbed the key from him and inserted it back in the lock of the driver's side and locked myself out. Having realized this, I caught myself firing up in even more of a rage and made a cool entrance into the coupe again. Confusion was overwhelming. I was having another spell. Fuck.

We drove up the coast, up about a mile or so, where I found my new home. I signed the lease that day and moved in the next. I called the garbage haulers to take everything in the old house, figuring I'd tell the landlord, "I'm out of there," when I got around to it. I just wanted to get away from all the lousy sex and bad women and people I had no clue how to relate to. I found the full-service apartment building I would probably collapse and croak in, where I was free to be completely alone and haunted only by thoughts and regret.

For the next month, I kept seeing Claudia, everywhere I went, everywhere! She'd come up with different identities, in different scenarios, driving different cars, romancing with different people, even speaking through other voices, but for the love of God, these women were all Claudia.

Georgie had another sales woman move in with him—the day they met—he was buying a new bed. It broke. They fell apart. Some kind of schizophrenia where you know you have it, but you're not allowed to be told you have it. It's like the opposite of schizophrenia. The doctors tell Georgie and me that all the chaos is normal. We're completely trapped, whether alone and together.

I look in the mirror and see myself at last, not the reflections and reactions of everybody *but* me.

38. THE NEW ACCESS TO FEED SOLITUDE

In the end, I wondered what all this meant.

This man was a hero. He was stuck in the misery of self. He didn't mean it to happen like that.

He was confused. He didn't have any conception of his identity. He wanted his own version of who he was. It didn't really matter what the others thought, in the long run.

His attempt to find a new access to feed his solitude implied a desire to feed something of his own. But the desire needed to be in control of the man, not the man in control of his desire. He wanted solitude.

Loneliness doesn't permit the expression of emotions to others. Instead, the emotions build up inside. Dark emotions come to the surface, from jealousy to hatred. He craved a resolution to his internal quest of self, his self alone. The access to grab hold of, or the mechanism, would need to come from something that was already there. His affection for knowledge of self could instinctively be turned around to express thoughtful affection to another person. He was ruled only by desire.

At first, he could not see others as the unique beings that they were. Others would remain only an opportunity to release negative feelings. A vacuum took the place where real communication should happen. By relaxing, taking things slow, and teasing himself, not expecting much, he could give time for his sensuality to grow, producing all the best connections to happiness. He hinted at things more than once, certain things. Some things kept coming out. He couldn't contain them. His mind was about to collapse.

Through his sense of nostalgia, his idea of his past made up for everything in the moment and beyond. He could finally release it and let it go for good. In other words, what has already happened, happened. The possibilities were what had meaning and substance.

What was probable was possible.

And in this new discovery, what really happened, what was imagined, what was perceived and experienced, were all genuine. They defined who this man found himself to be, as imperfect, as selfish, as selfless, and loving, as probable and as possible as anybody else.

He could become this man of other people, this affectionate, sympathetic, genuine individual.

We come to conclusions. We criticize. And we move on, as best as we can.

You're not alone.

Like I said in the beginning, you're doing just fine.

39. IS THIS A NEW BEGINNING?

The self-proclaimed narcissist and introvert, the author, has a realistic idea.

The skittish horse he is, he returns from the restroom. He takes his seat by the window in the front row. They still haven't announced any word about taking off yet. He's got a clear plastic cup of diluted OJ and a bottle of water. He downs them fast. He thinks how lucky he is to be sitting in first class. It was a free upgrade since his original flight never made it. It had mechanical problems.

A strange woman takes the aisle seat.

"Hi! You don't have to move. Don't worry. Don't move. I'm fine in the aisle."

"I prefer to be the one who moves out of the way for any bathroom-goers. I've got a big bladder, myself," Georgie says. "I just thought no one else was coming at this point."

"Don't worry about it. If you have to go, I'll move."

Don't worry about it? At least she wasn't some stinky old man. He looks at his overgrown fingernails, puts his hand out.

"My name's Georgie."

"Hi Georgie, I'm Maggie Fox."

She shakes his hand.

"Firm grip, Georgie."

"Yeah, I love to fly."

"Well, we've only got an hour or so. It's not bad."

"No, not bad at all."

A simple man is born. His name is Georgie Gust. He's a hallucination. He's all that I am today, for now, forever, for whatever reason. Sometimes there's just an overload of stimuli from the environment in the way of what we're after.

. . . What if Georgie kept in touch with this woman after the flight? What if he got her number and actually tried to continue knowing her?[51]

The flight hasn't even begun, and George's mind is racing. The events from the past year were still bombarding him with an

---

[51] *"Get out of my head, will you!?! I can handle this."*

urgent pressure. He sits there thinking. He remembers how pathetic things have become since the arrival of adulthood. He remembers the transition he could feel, literally, from an asshole little kid into a guilty and responsible abuser of waste. It's so easy to make fun of this guy! Now he doesn't feel like going home. Maggie's reading the current issue of *People Weekly*. They collect the pre-flight drinks and announce the takeoff procedures. Georgie looks out the window.

We trudge on, even through the storms, and we're fine. Everything's okay. We're here now, and everything's cool.

I never thought anything good would last, but I'm holding onto this—I can't slow down my pathetic little life just to think about things and regroup, and analyze. I was obsessed in a sexual obsession and a mind-bending paralysis. It was fun while it lasted . . .

Perplexity is that awareness you have at the worst moment of any mental suicide attempt. I'm experiencing it right now, and time is too heavy.

"Just slow down, and take it easy." I hear. "Stop thinking . . . just stop. Feel the blood run through your hands, your feet—your body. That's what matters. Now, get dressed and get out of here."

I'm awake and step outside. The sunrise is magnificent. The sand on the beach absorbs the bright light as it intensifies. I glance back for a moment and remember Georgie. I think of all the excuses I made, just to get over someone I thought was the perfect match for me—big mistake, but completely necessary. She was a nice woman, but we weren't made for each other.

So what, I'm alone now, and again, and it's all right now.

"Who's this voice you keep talking about?" Claudia asked when we were having dinner one night.

"They're just thoughts," I told her.

I think of Georgie. He can be overbearing sometimes.

Dear Claudia,

I know the voice is my own. I'm sorry it didn't work out between us. The rest is history.

Yours truly,

Benjamin J. Schreiber . . . Georgie Gust

40. MORE FROM "WASTE"

a novel by Benjamin J. Schreiber

I felt generally on edge, a bit anxious, a bit nonexistent, nervous, paranoid, and urgent—unlike yesterday, but still I bore it all. I finished another day, even with the recurring idea of "death" in the first person, in my head, every minute. The voices have dissipated, but perceptual hallucinations are rather present, though.

Looking at Heidi's (yes *Heide's*, I know, I realize it *is* Heide's, *not Claudia's*) place, next door, and the whole emotional situation, was extremely awkward for me from morning to night. They wanted to switch my meds, fuck, are they bending my mind back together? Have I taken the right pill? No, I've been off my meds, fucking psych meds for five days—as I'm thinking, half-asleep, the writer's block—it seems . . . it seems to have lifted. It's gone. I think I'm okay, in a way. I try, I try, I try . . .

I try to find things about her, about *Heide*, that are impure, detestable, and inferior. I'm wrong to judge her. I don't deserve to judge her. That's what I tell myself. No, fuck mind, I'm losing it, am I gaining a Super-Ego now? A mindful parent? I'm telling myself what's okay and what's not okay, I'm judging. But I do, I do judge her. I judge Heide. And I want to yell at her, scream at her, beat the crap out of her. In public, but I can't. I wasn't brought up that way. We couldn't just be "fuck buddies"—I talked my head off, trying to talk her into it. I wanted her that bad, and yet I couldn't even come with her at the end. I was jealous, she said, of her "abundant life." Fuck it. Fuck her. The way that Heidi can balance such chaos astounds me, even with her career. How does she do it? Her diatribe at Picarelli's about the "forbidden love affairs" that attract her, cause her to question them, yet, still make her feel good. Oh Ben, you're learning . . . "It's over!" . . . as you said it to her. She simply replies, "O.K." Legend has it O.K. stands for zero killed.

-Ben J. Schreiber

I send my short story in to one of the editors, by e-mail, fast. True story from the other day, I think it'll read as a commercially viable . . . something or other. I wish Kelly would understand.

I pray now, and I go to sleep. Women and angels, they hover over me still and quietly. I'm fucking loving it. Loving it, yeah . .

41. NOTATION: ON KELLY

Author's Note: I got another e-mail from Kelly. I think she likes me. Oh, wow, give me a fucking break already. Still wish she'd send a picture.

Dear Ben:

Fascinating work, such gritty, impersonal sex; it tears my heart in two. Nicely done. The problem though is that your reader cannot possibly follow your train of thought—too disjointed. You don't want to lose the reader. How about a through-line, lead your reader by the hand as it were. Does that make sense? Oh, and the quote, it includes one-on-one, just like you asked. Best of luck with this. Let me know how else I can help. -Kelly

Yeah, Kelly's okay. Better than Kevin at Gold Hand:

First off, no, not the "Trish" piece.[52] Too clichéd. Perhaps the main storyline is rooted like this: The romantically doomed neighbors, Georgie and Claudia, are an attractive couple who, having rushed their passion in each other in the very beginning, split up. They're both inflicted with a low sense of self-worth of which their actions show.

To self,

I love this whole business she has of saying, "Does that make sense?" She's dominant. I want to be her servant, her slave boy, her boy toy, her big beef. She must have a habit of asking if that "makes sense." I can just hear it. That little quirk she's got, surely. But on the novel, I'm thinking over a coffee mug filled with espresso. Ten minutes have passed and . . . nothing.

. . . When I broke up with "the real Claudia: Heidi."

-Ben J. Schreiber

---

[52] Note: Please see next chapter, FYI/FMI. —*Your Ben Forever*

42. INTERLUDE

Trish

The alternative e-mailer at the independent video store...

I gave the owner a deposit to quote my broken video camera, but they were ready to rip me off more than the lousy ten dollars.

I started to think about the owner who called me with the verdict. I was still in bed. $200.

The camera only cost me that much. I needed to get it back, untouched. I didn't care about the deposit anymore. Besides, it was the young lady behind the counter who was fascinating my heart and my mind. I didn't know why until I stepped back inside the next day, jangling the bells on the front door. I had nothing really important going on at the time. I felt like being social, and I saw my match. I thought I could fake being real confident. Then I'd have her.

I needed to gear up some plastic emotions. Felt the need to withdraw from the store owner first, the back-ender. I don't like penetration. He was trying to pull a foreign stunt at the local video shop. Perhaps he'd take some interest in me, constructive criticism from the perspective of a potential client.

But he took the day off. Sent in some pipsqueak little girl to cover for him, having trained her with the art of how to rip off customers by means of deception.

After all, the same thing happened to the guy in front of me, in line. He got ripped off, too, standing uptight but quite passive before the part-time chick kicking back, back behind the counter.

I called her Trisha. She looked like a Trish. It was that chick, Trish and me. And we had all the time in the world, all alone, just the two of us.

"Behave yourself," the voice in my head was muttering. But this girl looked familiar, this hot-blooded punk rocker. New Age, neo-slacker, occultist wannabe with her feet up, up at the front. But she was cute.

Okay. I might've got the cam back and rented a dirty movie from such a slutty cashier, letting her see what excited me, smelly feet and *Gothika*, femdom and arse play.

I dug her. Boy, did she dig me, I thought.

My thought process became sick and surreal. I was fired up sexually. Garbled thinking in fragments, this beauty queen, this fantasy, my nightmare of her reality. She haunted my head with an eerie sensation of thrill. She seemed mean and angry but loads of fun, fun, fun.

Trish must've sparked lots of other interested eyes, too. She might've described herself differently, though, when she wrote. When I wrote like this to describe one like that, she'd probably beg to differ. She probably knew herself better than I did.

So what did she have to say about herself? Surely it's all been written down in her journal, a little black hardcover notebook. I knew I'd better watch my mouth. I could have been the source of her next free thought. I might have supplied this gothic poet with her next new big idea or something, something to tickle her silly with glee. Something she'd scribble down in her little notebook, observations of life as seen through the naked eyes of the video rental chick, a Celtic cross beside the title.

She wasn't intimidating when I walked inside. Anytime I might have, except that time. Who'd be sitting there eating up a hefty dose of time as it wrapped around her? Who else? Yup, she was relaxing while others were tense, thinking, drinking an energy drink. Thinking about how her job made her feel like she was really living the whole Kevin Smith's *Clerks* breakthrough cult flick thing and how weird that seemed to her and that in her idleness, she was really growing as a person, sometimes, and, "Ya know, like all that corporate conspiracy, and those poor disgruntled rich people and their quality of life, of lies, or not. Or not having enough money to pay the rent? . . . All that culture and society, and excess of human expression? It's all, kind of, just like, okay sometimes. I don't know, less room for error or something."

"You go, girl!"

"Yeah, life is good." (I know *that's* in a book.) But like she was saying, "So what if I'm somehow intellectually overqualified to well, hang out a while, meet some interesting people, you know, and dress how I want. They don't mind too much black here, or here. Heh-heh (laughs). *Scarface* is on the VCR at my disposal." (She quickly unveiled that "Am I Guilty or

202

What?" non-twinkling disfigured smile that said dumbfounded, as if "What else could I ask for in life?" [Adding] "Any film I want for that matter" [film not video].)

"The cute guys? I get a pretty good idea of who they are by the choices they make here. (Hint, hint.) In a way, life's no paradox for me. I mean, c'mon. I'm not complaining."

"Tell me about the owner of this joint who wants to rip me off to fix my video camera. Tell me!" I commanded.

"Oh, my boss? He's cool."

Trish blew a bubble of pink chewing gum. It popped.

"That's it! That's the end of you! You rebel!"

Fuckin' bubble gum girl, fuckin' Valley Girl, fuckin' Trish, she was such a cute little soldier in her own private anarchist world. I couldn't bear anything about her. My fantasy of her ended abruptly. With all that was swarming in my head, I couldn't bear to think of any real moments I might have had with her. I told her I was in the wrong place, that I was sorry, that I had the wrong address. I was trying to do something, trying to find love.

What a way to fuckin' try.

43. 3:05 AM

I still can't fall asleep, although I'm tired and have been tired. I want to be knocked out. I took Valerian root and melatonin as well.

Have I mentioned Heidi?

I find myself trying to fall asleep before her and wake up before her, by watching the lights at her place. I keep failing. My obsession ends with her now. We are different people. What bothered me most though was this incompletion of my fantasy of her reality as a lesbian with Sara. Heidi loves her. They kiss. They make out. They hold hands. All in private. Sara bites Heidi's thighs. They leave cuts and bruises on each other. They play with sex toys together. Dildos. They kiss passionately and with love. Monogamy, loving one person, is a farce. True love is not true. The fantasy of them never turned into something tangible for me. It was so in-the-dark, and still is—even more so now—so forbidden and out in the open. She did treat me "with respect and dignity." Was I too weak to accept her affairs? Is that it? Too jealous?

I denied my love for Amanda and any other lusts while with her. How can I improve myself—becoming less susceptible and more adaptive? I cannot sleep. The cleaners come tomorrow. I've got a meeting at three. Church, Sunday morning.

"Benjamin, stay in the now."

I should try therapy again—for real, hypnosis. I need a plan so that my life becomes its own story. I'll play the lead character. I need personal goals. A mission statement. I need a change. I'm lonely. I'm stuck.

#

11:25 AM . . . Again, Heidi called twice today. She knew my weakness and didn't respect my boundaries. Yet, it ended nicely. I felt she was confused, loony, addicted herself, and genuine. I don't know what she wants. I love her anyway. Why not? We agreed she'll call me in a month to see where we both are. The 28th of March? We'll see.

She really misses me, but no I love you and no proposal for something steady.

A good book or story idea? How I can't get over her.

Love, Ben J. Schreiber

44. BEN AND POPS

Georgie looks down at us from above, somewhere, someplace. He must not have been fully integrated into the *life-with-me*—with Ben, the genius. Georgie was not needed, and I was not the full-fledged narcissist in need of another self, not yet. I was still young, before sixth grade. I'd recently been armed with the popular labels, attention deficit and Tourette's, and Moms was on vacation, on a cruise, with my sister Lenore, of course.

"You always ruin every vacation we take together, Ben." I heard as they'd leave the front door for a silly Carnival cruise, American Princess, etc.

Later, I'd drift away from them, from Sis and Moms, and Moms would tell me, "It would be really nice to have you back in the family."

I'd take her remarks as: "You should be back with us."

What she probably meant was,

1) "I won't cop to anything, you weren't abused,

2) "I know I can't have you back . . . I'm sorry, sorry . . . no!

3) "You're an out-of-control brat and I hate you . . ."

Something like that . . .

God, that woman makes me angry. I hate her, I don't want her to leave . . . Borderline this, crisis-after-crisis that. Georgie could feel the living, colorful beauty of the immaculate synthesis, a by-product of fear, Doctor C calls it, the immaculate built-up split inside me, for afterwards, Georgie would need to take it all in, swallow and deal with it. Maybe he'd end up in a tap dancing class.

Tap-and-dance to the beats of bologna.

He was looking over at me. I was eating a pizza and staring at the television set with the occasional glance over at my father. We were together. Father had nuked up some microwave popcorn. They'd just started to pre-install microwave units into the newer condos in America, and we were in Utah, only an hour's drive (an hour's drive, Lord) to the slopes, the small ski village of Sandy, Utah. This boys' vacation away from "home" happened before Pops broke the bank, and we were all a lot more modest than we are today.

It was a father-son trip. We flew by plane, in coach, into Salt Lake City, and we did a heavy ton of driving, music on, memory-building music. The snow was crystallizing on the boughs of the trees, snowy white pines, even red cedar, young deer running loose in the nearby state parks; the purest sensation of adolescent nostalgia was causing tiny shivers in my spine, causing my thin, little-boy arms to quiver.

Snowed in as we were, I was with my father, watching a rented copy of *Raising Arizona* on VHS, just after the BetaMaxes became obsolete, I can't remember. Most of the best parts of growing up have dulled in my mind, and any magic was quelled.

By the end of that first Saturday night, my dad and I took a soak in the outdoor Jacuzzi, the steam rising up and over the wall thermometer, which indicated the temperature was twenty degrees, maybe fifteen; like I said, I don't remember all that well.

All I know is that I fell asleep on the couch that night, and we were able to hit a couple of slopes on Sunday. Pops took me to the top of a few of the black diamond slopes; I was kind of challenged to race down, Pops right behind me, even without the agility I had then as a kid.

Pops wiped out at the bottom. I wiped out, too.

We had fun while it lasted before I would go back home to Mother. Dad would leave the house shortly afterwards.

I'd never have another father-son experience quite like it. I guess that's why it means so much to me now, as faded as the memory is. It was. It isn't.

45. ALTER-EGO CLAUDIA: GEORGIE'S NIGHTMARE AT NOON

Since the new medication regimen seems to be working and the writer's block seems to be done, I feel rushed. That's strange. So, Georgie spends a full day *de-Claudia-nizing* his otherwise crappy little house. His living room is now the small studio where he just sits around without the comfort of having any furniture. He lets the monotony of the hour take control of him, wishing for the next day to begin and this current day to end.

Georgie is dilly-dallying on any business of finding a new place to live. Starting early in the morning for once, he cleans out his house out completely once the idea of Claudia is removed through the process of thought-stopping. All the enlarged photographs and framed letters and notes have been locked inside a storage unit in the next town. His collection of vintage Pez dispensers, vanilla-scented candles, and novelty gifts are now locked in hell, locked in Georgie's mind. The candles he got for his birthday kept like new for too long. They're now being burned.

Get your gun, Georgie. As if there was any gun. Load it with love. Shoot your fucking dick off.

"But not tonight, Georgie," is what she says, over and over again, fucking around with him.

Here comes the heat.

The hot light from the bleeding sun is sucked into the camera. We're inside the dark studio, with all that's left of Georgie's old pad, somewhere in Los Angeles. The blinds are closed. The sunlight bleeds through them horizontally. Georgie is thirty years old. He's shivering cold, scruffy-faced, holding a can of mace, lines of coke on the floor. He suffocates in smoke by the door. Lit candles surround him. The lights are dim. Ten ashtrays are occupied with smoldering cigarettes and joints. They give off loaves of white smoke into the still air.

Georgie is wrapped in a blanket. He's self-aware.

The Brit-Invasion pop music of your choice is muffled but loud. Alternative music follows.

Georgie's a one-man crowd.

The static of a radio dial turning. These are the sounds inside Georgie's head burning. He's drenched in sweat. For the first time, he's in debt. He can barely suck in a breath of fresh air, much less any filthy air.

Women's panties with their rank sex odor and an array of sex toys are scattered on the floor. There's more—her notes, her gifts, and dead flowers. Seconds pass like hours. Georgie clenches a cup of water and nearly drowns in it. He chokes and likes the sound of it.

We're at the beach. Georgie's wrapped in satin bed sheets. The moonlight illuminates Georgie and Claudia.

She's forty, forty-one. She never gave away her real age to anyone. Georgie and she are posing for pictures, all happy and shit. He's got a cigarette lit. He thinks the long beach is a huge public ashtray.

They run around on the sand, playfully. Georgie remembers this as he tells me. Claudia dips her big feet in the water. Georgie smiles at the sight of her. He tries to lick her feet, but she dunks his face in the water instead, dismissing any licks or kisses.

Often, she'd dismiss his advances while in bed. He wondered if she'd ignore him if they'd been wed.

His head is bobbing in and out of the water with her force. He spits out sand.

Claudia laughs with mischief. She takes Georgie's hand.

We're in the middle of an empty parking lot, near Claudia's piece-of-shit '91 Honda. The CD player's on high, more music.

Georgie and Claudia dance together with the big Discount Clearance Store banner in the background, total suburbia.

The fire alarm's blaring high. We're back in the studio where Georgie's beating himself up.

"Somebody save me!"

At the door to an apartment across the street, a woman's voice. "Come in."

Georgie, blowing bubble gum, opens the door, only to find Claudia kissing another woman. It's that Sara chick, Claudia's alcoholic lesbian lover, the mystery woman of misery, now in the flesh. I can't see her. She must not be real either. Claudia looks over. Her eyes widen majestically.

"Georgie! Hi, Princess!"

210

She hallucinates Sara, Georgie hallucinates Claudia, and I hallucinate Georgie. Claudia and Sara stand topless in the center of the room. Claudia's in latex gear.

There's a small audience witnessing their fetish desires, Greg, fifty-five, long, white hair, puff-belly, fuzzy navel, wedding band, an oaf. He's with his wife, twenty-five, skinny, boney, looking innocent, wearing a gold cross charm. They watch the woman-to-woman make-out scene like stiffs sitting side-by-side, hands on their laps. They don't flinch a muscle.

Georgie tics. Claudia sees his neck jerk and his eyes roll. She waves Georgie to come closer.

"Just don't come too close."

Georgie swallows his chewing gum. He can't take his eyes off the very woman he concocted in his mind. She kicks off her pumps.

"Tell me a little more about yourself, Georgie. I want to get to know you," she says.

Georgie grabs one of her shoes, smells the vinegary sponge of the soles. Greg and his wife smirk.

Embarrassed and ashamed, Georgie starts to run away.

"Don't leave!" Claudia shouts. Then her voice softens. "I want to introduce you, Georgie."

Georgie hesitates.

"Fuck you. I fucking love you. You're fucking with my mind again."

Claudia remarks, "I'm not fucking with your mind. Damn it, Georgie! I told you I wouldn't do that. I told you!" The fire alarm next door is still firing off. Sound over noise.

Claudia dashes out of her front door and into Georgie's.

Georgie's still sitting in the middle of the room. The alarm is louder. We hear Claudia perfectly though. Georgie looks up.

She explains, "I'm just a habit, Georgie, an addiction. I've got my life together. It's all figured out!" Georgie's heard that before.

His eyes are desperate, ready to give up completely. He knows all of this is only a matter of his imagination.

His imagination is mine.

She tapes his mouth shut and cuffs his wrists to his ankles. His chest sticks out. Georgie fails to restrain her.

We're at a sushi restaurant in town. Georgie and Claudia are having dinner together. Georgie hands her a pink rose. They walk hand-in-hand, together on the sidewalk in the center of town. She kisses him. He pinches her ass.

Claudia continues explaining herself in the studio.

"Georgie, I was using you when it was convenient for me. I'm a woman, Georgie. I'm from another planet. I never even told you that I loved you, God!"

Suddenly Claudia can't breathe right.

They start to fight physically. Georgie does his best to defend himself while still caught up within the chains. He looks like a wounded rocking horse. Claudia finds this amusing.

"Georgie, you're fighting! Look at you go. Let go!"

Georgie makes muffled sounds.

Claudia mimics him. "Stop! Stop! What are you trying to say, baby?" She puts a stranglehold on him. She kisses him hard while he tries to hold back. Claudia pulls out a rubber from Georgie's back pocket. She licks the tape over his mouth.

Georgie squeaks.

She undoes his pants, coughing from the smoke in the air. She puts her face up close.

"Just don't touch my breasts. Don't even ask." Then she realizes. "Oh, you can't anyway. Fine!"

She undoes her bottom and tosses the condom away. It seems like everything's in slow motion for a second.

Georgie's still locked up and suffocating.

Claudia sees that he's trying to say something. She undoes the tape on his mouth.

He's out of breath. "You fucking whore bitch cunt!"

Claudia laughs. "Good." And tapes him back up. "I'm a social worker."

Everything's still and quiet for a moment.

"Now, get me pregnant! I want to abuse you, just like you wanted. I love it. I don't love you."

She's fucking Georgie, fuckin' raping him. She rips off the tape from his lips.

Georgie yells, "Get off! Get off!"

"I am. I am getting off. I have complete control, now, cum inside me, Georgie, cum inside me, slut."

212

The phone rings. Police officers are pounding at the door. Somebody else must have called them, probably Rocky, the feminine florist who lives next door. Georgie cums hard, unloading himself deep inside her, hating it, feeling shattered and corrupted.

Another day, Claudia and Georgie are making out on the sofa, before the day he had the big rage attack and the shit hit the fan. Georgie says, "I love you."

He hears, "Thanks."

Georgie is on the phone with her. "I have thirty of your messages saved on my voicemail!" says Claudia. "I like listening to them on my way to work. Wherever I go, I get to smile."

She's on her way to the car. It's parked outside. She forgets exactly where.

Georgie's watering his lawn. He tries to break up with her before it's all long and drawn out, but Claudia suspects his weakness. She smiles with winced eyebrows.

"I'm not letting you go that easily," she says.

Back in the studio, Georgie is entirely wiped out.

Claudia unlocks and untapes him. She leaves, without an expression to ponder.

Georgie blurts out, "It never ends!"

Claudia looks back. "I'll call you." She shuts the door behind her.

Georgie knows she won't call.

The smells of wine and weed evaporate off Claudia's deep beauty. She sneaks back into the studio, coming up behind Georgie and holding a camouflage shotgun. She blows his head to shreds with ten explosive shots.

"Get out of your head, you sick fucking twist. Love is a lie."

The screen fades quickly to red, blending to black.

46. EASY STEPS TO A PERFECT PEDICURE (DÉJÀ VU)

I take just one of the pills, and I remember Georgie, when I moved out west in the last week of October. I remember it differently, still fuzzy, still a little surreal. Shit, Pasadena and all of Los Angeles County were blisteringly hot, and I was working up an uncomfortable sweat. I heard screaming and yelling. It was Halloween, and Claudia, who lived across the street, broke up with her girlfriend. Her lover flew out the door as Claudia chased her down the sidewalk.

All the little kids were excited to see the upcoming catfight, all in their G-rated costumes. Some were frightened as their parents and chaperones held them back from any danger.

I watched from my front window. Claudia slapped her ex right across the face, and she went down. It took only one blow until she lay on the ground, slurring something back like, "Dicksucker!" The neighborhood kids in our little yuppie town, just bordering the San Marino mansions, were eager for my dollar-bills-instead-of-candy setup at the front door. Claudia watched with a bottle of wine after her lover finally took off for good.

Within a couple of minutes, she looked at her watch and twitched. Dashing from her front patio, she came to mine. The children scattered as I smiled nervously at my new neighbor. She was prancing wide-eyed like she had something on the tip of her tongue to tell me. Her face was covered with red lipstick kisses. She leaned over my front fence.

"Come here. Come here."

I stepped in closer. "Hi," I said.

"Hi, neighbor, I'm Claudia. I know we haven't met yet, but, well, you probably just saw, yeah, my girlfriend and I were on pretty thin ice together."

"Yeah. Sorry to know that," I explained.

She looked me in the eyes.

I looked down at her bare feet. Her big pale feet. Her perfect long, little toes. Her adolescent pink nail polish, halfway scraped off. She was about forty or so. Her hair was crazy and red. Her animated personality was wild like my imagination. After all, she saw me looking down at her floor floaters and took me out of my pathetic, horny little spell of intoxicating sensations. I felt close to her, but I was no sooner interrupted by her soft voice. It was sweet and a little raspy.

"I forgot. There's this Halloween party I'm going to be late to, up in Hawthorne. I need my nails done, and my girlfriend, well my ex, I guess, was going to do my feet."

A teepee started to build in my pants. "What are you going as?"

"A hooker."

My balls started to ache like they needed a bucket of ice. I repeated what she said in my head a couple of times in disbelief.

Claudia was a bombshell.

#

Paula Cole's erotic music was playing softly on Claudia's cheap little CD player. "Feelin' Love."

Lots of candles were lit, mostly vanilla scented. I was wearing a light blue dress shirt with a loose tie and ripped denims.

Claudia was naked.

"I can't believe you've never given a girl a pedicure."

"Believe. I'm a virgin, Claudia."

She sat on her toilet bowl. I held her foot in my lap. My cock was feeling really left out, but I liked feeling this agony, at least for the moment. This woman didn't even know my name. She looked down at me. We were still complete strangers, and I thought she was a lesbian. I questioned myself whether or not my boner was a bad thing. Were we being sensual? Good God damn. You bet we were!

Claudia handed me a container of Tiger Balm. She asked me not to put my fingers in between her toes because she's really ticklish. So I closed my eyes and massaged her feet for a couple of minutes, which passed like hours.

"Mmm. That's so relaxing. It tingles. It's warm." She moaned.

I removed her old pink nail polish with store-brand nail polish remover. Claudia said I was a quick learner.

216

I was then instructed to fill a tub of warm water so I did and then added some salts with a vanilla-scented foot soak. She soaked them for about five minutes until she fell asleep. I didn't want to wake her so I removed her beautiful, clean, pasty-white feet from the water and patted off all the excess water. I loaded the palms of my hands with a hefty dose of body lotion she'd stolen from some hotel before starting to massage her feet from the toes down to her heels. Her feet twitched a little. My eyes were closed with hers.

She had these pumice stones laid out by the sink. I was familiar with what they did from watching pedicures being done in beauty parlors, so I dabbed some more lotion on the stones and very gently buffed any area I felt needed softening. Her feet were cotton-soft by this time. I kissed them, hoping Claudia wouldn't wake up. I could see this sad smile on her face. I passed it off as part of a dream she was dissolving in. She was such a da Vinci angel. She was heavenly and peaceful. I wanted her to be mine.

I dabbed more lotion on her feet, covered them in large plastic baggies, wrapped warm towels around her feet, and let them sit for fifteen minutes. She woke up.

"Well done. Well done, Mister." She smiled. "Would you bring me a glass of that red wine from the kitchen?" she asked me with the most pleasant of voices.

After I returned with her wine, she lit a joint and was inhaling seductive hits from it. She offered me a drag with a gesture. I nodded in the negative. "Good boy."

Removing the baggies, I massaged the remainder of the lotion into her feet. Then I buffed her toenails furiously, starting to have a little fun. My boner softened a bit. We laughed together.

"What color would you like?" I asked.

"What do you think? What would look good on me? Say, if you could have my toes?" And up went my groin stick again. Precum was leaking out. I could feel it. I touched it for a second, and she busted me.

"What are you doing?" She laughed.

"Nothing."

I went on to carefully paint her nails with a base coat, her toes separated with cotton balls. When they dried, I colored her toenails with two coats of Hooker Blue and was about to leave so I could go back home and jerk off as fast as I could. I was sweaty with guilt, shame, and frustration.

"Neighbor, wait!"

"I gotta go. Sorry."

"But I'm late for the party," she exclaimed.

I stopped in my tracks.

"I want to congratulate you on what a great job you did on my pedicure, and on such short notice."

I smiled, still horny as all hell.

"Now it's your turn."

My face shot that "Am I in a dream?" look.

She had me sit on the same toilet seat she was on. And she took the floor where I was. She remained naked and told me to get naked with her.

I undressed slowly and sat down in front of her with my huge boner at attention.

"This has become your night, after all. I need to thank you, neighbor. I need to welcome you to the neighborhood. What's your name, anyway?" she asked.

"George . . . no, Ben."

"You silly thing. Make up your mind."

"Just call me Ben."

"You're young."

"I'm thirty, but I admire older women. Mature women. Women older than me, for that matter," I confessed.

"And you like feet?" she asked respectfully.

Before I could say anything, her freshly pedicured feet were making their way up my thigh and gently touching my balls and shaft. I felt queasy, sick, dizzy, in heaven, in agony. I could see right into her crotch. Her shaved pussy was dripping wet. Her vagina looked so lonely. Within a minute, I couldn't take it any longer, and I demanded, "Claudia, you've got to make me cum. Fast. Please. Make me cum. I promise I won't ever ask you again in such a selfish hurry. Please!"

Her feet started stroking my tall, erect cock up and down as it looked up at my face boiling all my love sap as it was about to explode.

"Do you want to cum in my mouth?" Claudia asked.

218

"On your feet. Just like that. Don't stop. Don't stop." I begged.

"Are you close?" And before I could answer, her feet were splashed with my white nut. To join me, Claudia masturbated her clit in a restless fury and squirted all over the work I had done on her feet. I rubbed it in with my big hands, massaging what was left of her new feet.

We nodded out together.

The next morning, Halloween was over, and we had to get up, get out of the bathroom, and get off to work. We could skip any showering that morning as the leftover aroma of sex on our skin became our private souvenirs.

#

I knew I wanted to see this woman again . . . and again, in Long Beach. Strangely, I knew I would strike up a relationship with Heidi Berillo in Long Beach, and that said, we'd both be involved with catastrophic love affairs beyond our dignities, beyond our distance . . . a solid premise for the big novel, a living, colorful beauty and a local borderline personality, or would that be two personalities? Or three? Or four?

A parallel universe. A universal reflection of personality itself. Lord, hear our prayer.[53]

I'm making, fucking making it, man.

Swimming back to the surface . . . at least back to the doc.

---

[53] I've never had a client like Ben. Yes, I've had rich clients, creative clients, clients who've been sexually assaulted, but I've never had one quite like Ben. He intrigues me, particularly the invention of Georgie, who is the repository for all Ben's emotions, particularly as those emotions pertain to his (Georgie's?) sexuality. Those emotions range from desire to lust to shame and self-loathing. *Objective: heal the split between the two.*

47. REHAB AND MOTHER

Dr. C hangs on my every word about the robbery and rehab. I know she doesn't want to hang on to every word, but the thing is she can't resist a story of mayhem and criminality. No one can. You learn when you're a writer that violence, criminal behavior, sex, and drugs—all of it, any of it, sells. And that's all I'm doing is selling Dr. C a story, hoping she buys it.

"Does that mean you're dishonest?" Dr. C asks.

I think—I pretend to think—and shake my head 'no.'

"Not dishonest," I say. "Not exactly. No. I wouldn't say that."

"Then what would you say, Ben?"

I think—pretend to think—and say, "Now, well . . . I'm not exactly sure. What would you say, Dr. C?"

She smiles, says nothing.

Of course, what else could she do?

She wants me to jump in, fill the silence with my own thoughts, my own impressions. I sink into the chair, refuse to play that game. Several seconds pass. Several long silent seconds. Finally:

"Did I tell you my mother visited me in rehab?" I ask.

Silently, Dr. C shakes her head 'no.'

"Want me to tell you about it?" I ask.

"If that's what you want," Dr. C says.

Typical psychiatric bullshit.

"Well, now, Dr. C, if I didn't want to tell you about my mother visiting, I wouldn't have brought it up in the first place, would I have?"

"You sound angry, Ben. Are you angry?"

"Not me. Uh-uh. No, sir. Anger is a waste. Why get angry? Be happy."

I laugh. Dr. C does not join in.

I sigh and begin my newest story: My mother and her short, tight curly hair, and her grotesque, out-of-shape, obese body. This is my greatest fear: that one day I'll wake up looking just like her, and then I'll have to kill myself.

Dr. C smiles sardonically and asks if Georgie is patterned more on myself or more on my mother.

It's a stupid question and one I refuse to answer.

Then Dr. C asks if I enjoyed my mother's visits in rehab. Ha-ha. Like anyone could enjoy a visit with my mother. My mother has one of those East Coast voices, loud and nasal; she is always clearing her throat, and if I didn't know better, I'd swear she has Tourette's. She is an Episcopalian; however, with her talent for guilt, I always suspected she was a closeted Catholic.

"Interesting," Dr. C says.

"What?" I ask.

"All of it," she says, then smiles enigmatically.

Christ, I hate enigmatic smiles.

I continue: My mother was a firm believer in regular church attendance, even required that I become an altar boy. Why she went to church or what she thought she gained was never clear to me. She certainly didn't learn to love in church, at least not in any New Testament way. No, not my mother. My mother was quick to hit—spare the rod, spoil the child—and she brought that up when she visited me at Valley View.

She sat on the side chair in my room, her legs crossed primly at the ankle, and cried.

"I just don't know what I did wrong, Benjy. Tell me. I'm a reasonable woman. What did I do?"

"And what did you tell her?" Dr. C asks.

I think about that. I don't pretend to think, I do think. And what the hell—I don't remember. I've never remembered any of the things I've told my mother, only the things she's told me.

"And what were those things?" Dr. C asks.

"Stand up straight. Don't slouch. Be normal. Stop ticking like that."

"Must have been hard to do all those things."

It must have been, but I don't remember; I don't remember any of the things I did. Did I obey? Rebel? Why can't I remember? Why can't I fucking remember?

Dr. C reaches for my hand. I pull back.

"Psychiatrists who touch their patients are suspect in my book. Sorry."

I get to my feet. "Well, Dr. C," I tell her, my voice rich, cultured, melodious—everything Dr. C is not.

"Well," I repeat. "Same time Tuesday?"

Dr. C nods. And I leave. I am so out of there.[54]

---

[54] 10/25/06: Pt. relayed reason for therapy: Bank robbery in Pasadena. Question re: robbery attempt to be placed in rehab? Pt. discussed mother, described her as loud. No discussion of sexual abuse. Correlation b/twn literary device & mother?

48. END THE VIOLENCE

My mother was always stressed. Always, because she had this thing for talking in extremes, being in extremes—always mad, never good.

At the dinner table, Moms, Sis, and me:

"Shut up and eat your peas, before I give you a fucking beating you'll never forget."

She and my dad, my sister and I, even the poor little dog we lived with, "Punkin," a tiny, black and gray Shih Tzu, adopted from the county fair, she'd eat her shit, frozen with wafts of steam coming off in the dead of our suburban winters. She'd, in turn, be so maliciously tortured by my mother. She'd say, "Bad dog, Punkin, bad dog," and whack the living daylights out of her. As Punkin aged, she became more and more skittish, the more Moms would tell me how skittish I was becoming. And we'd yell, yes, typical American Family yelling fights.

"Where do you think you're going?" asked Moms.

"Boarding school."

"Where?"

"Boarding school."

"Hmm, where again?"

"Boarding school, Mom, and Dad agreed it was okay; I've waited for this. Let me go. I want to go."

After each time I responded, "Boarding school," I submitted to her fat, whacking hand across my pale-and-stubbly teenaged face, blood out of my nose and Rudolph ears.

Like, "Where?"

"Boarding school."

Whack!

"Where?"

"Fuck you!"

Whack! No wedding ring, just a white gold with six-carat diamond ring chipping at my ear and only-to-cherish teen sideburns, well, the left one.

"Where?"

Until I yelped, "Fuck you, Moms-bitch, fucking Phillips Exeter in New Hampshire, cunt rag," and I swung one huge pounding down onto her nose, which, click, snap, would break and bleed, and Moms would never hit me again.

I ended up somewhere else for school and carried all my familial baggage with me through college and through every torn relationship where I was to be broken-hearted from being a fucking Pinto-Honky-Worthless-Piece-of-Shit who needed a new mother.

That's what love means to me.

Moms was obsessed with the family and our family secrets, sexual love and beatings, and things that'll be keeping my novel off the bestseller list, because I've taken my hits and stings and things with an urgent "I'm the victim, and fuck you, Dr. Phil," so they're much too urgent to be written out with any care and thought. It was just bad.

Moms had knickknacks around the house, porcelain elephants, collectibles; she was artistic by nature, though nothing ever took off for her, and she couldn't read, as I can't. The two of us together might have gotten through one regular book in our lives and that would be her, no, maybe me. I don't know.

She burned food. She was a Little League mom. She loved me but didn't know how to show it. My mother was obsessed with sex. She liked to appliqué life-size, anatomically correct penises on my sister's Cabbage Patch Dolls and on one of my own. The penises wouldn't have been all that bad if she had done the same thing with an occasional vulva or pudendum now and then, but she didn't. It was just penises. She was obsessed. With my penis as well; she liked to play what she called 'groineology,' wherein she'd grab me high on the thigh, right on the groin, and dig in as hard and tight as she could, her blood red nails leaving imprints on my skin. "Groineology, Bennie," she'd say, laughing all the while. "Kiss me on the lips," she demand, even at age twenty-five, turn yourself into your dad and into me, as the victim of my own mom and dad, they *Mother Dearest*ed me, which is why I now collect the movie memorabilia, in fact.

Oh, and she hit me. Did I mention how much she hit me?

My great-grandmother's (father's mother's) last words to me were, "Oh yeah, Rose, boy, Benjamin, the way she used to hit you."

And she died peacefully that night in her bedroom, at ninety-nine.

Georgie tells me to watch Dr. Phil, as Dr. Phil's voice is in your head telling you to let go and fucking gimme a break, you lousy, lazy, beautiful little baby.

. . . Seek help soon.

49. ACCIDENTAL BIRTH

My Life by Benjamin J. Schreiber:

Mine was an accidental birth. I was supposed to have been born in June 1968—the year of the huge Democratic Convention in Chicago. Instead I was born in 1976—our Bicentennial. I think all my problems stem from that birth confusion.

Look at it: 1968, the hippies, radicals, and subversives were on the upswing; by 1976, the tide had turned. Patriotism was back. In a big way.

I grew up in Suffern, New York, three houses away from Mahwah, New Jersey. Again, I think that's added to my confusion; my schizophrenia if you will. It's what I figure the Navajo out in the Four Corners go through. Shit, you could be in four states at one time, instead of only the two I was always in, remain in: New York, New Jersey. Happy, sad. Angry, loving. Paranoid, brave. Kind.

A real asshole, I think, when I'm in the self-loathing mode. I lose more and more control of my emotions, the images become more and more powerful. The split, the split. Where's Dr. C's pager number? I can't wait until tomorrow.[55]

---

[55] Dr. C: Session Notes (pressed for time): Ben breaks my heart, shatters it in a million pieces, breaks it in ways I never knew it could break, and yet the more it breaks, the more he is able to affect me. I should refer Ben to another therapist. I am losing my objectivity.

50. SECOND SKINS WITH FOOTNOTES

Dr. C asks, "You've mentioned Heidi before, Ben; why don't you tell me more about her?"

"Heidi is my obsession. My Perplexity. She is the woman who changed my life and not in a good way. She brings back Georgie, who hasn't been around since Mrs. Petite. Claudia is Georgie's Heidi."

#

As an adult, I pleasure myself with the latex wrapped around me, snug, warm, wet with saliva. There's no mess to clean up when I'm through . . .

. . . All that time, I was trying to be safe and doubling up meant security to me. I moved out of town a few months later and never saw Claudia Nesbitt again. She fucked me, and she fucked with my head. I loved her, in my own twisted way. She wouldn't really ever change. Who was I kidding?[56]

#

I see her everywhere. Claudia, Marilyn, Ashley, everywhere. She's the essence of every woman I come in contact with. She never ends, like a photocopy of a photocopy.

Talk about an obsessive-compulsive personality . . . This fantasy world in my head, in my heart; it's becoming my reality. I can't seem to get over her . . . and I only met her once.

"Am I turning into psycho-boy?"

Where's the simplicity I once knew. How might I regain that?

"This shall all pass," I hear. "You'll be just fine in the long run."[57]

---

[56] Dr. C sits back. "That's quite a story, Ben. Interesting you tell it through Georgie's eyes." I stand up, make as to leave. I've never liked therapy, never needed it, do it only to appease my father, the police. The social workers who think I have a problem. Other than the Tourette's, the schizoaffective, and bipolar shit. I laugh inappropriately at the thought. Dr. C notices. "So," she says, "what's your primary memory from when you were little, Ben?" After a short pause: "There was a jogger," I tell her. "Jogger in the winter. Same clothes. You must really sweat when you jog."

Christmas: I've read that there is such a thing as the Christmas Blues, the realization that you haven't gotten everything you wanted. Never happened to me. Not from the time I was ten, not from the time my father made his first million. "And what did you want?" Dr. C asks. I respond without thinking, "To be normal." Instantly, my eyes fill with tears.

51. BENEVOLENT GEORGIE

There is a genuine goodness to Georgie, as unsacred and as unwholesome as he might otherwise seem to be. Yes, he does see beauty in every woman, he gives out money, he's religious in the truest sense of the word, he holds people in the highest regard. It's I who have the racial tics, then? I'm the one who lets people cut in line. No, Georgie. He holds the door open for everyone, even if for ten minutes, as they all pile out at rush hour. It's Georgie who carries packages. On his way to Dr. C's, Georgie buys food for the homeless and hands it out, carefully deciding by their homely looks who gets what. Georgie forgives everyone, more or less, even when they don't deserve forgiveness.

The sun beats down on Georgie's arms as he walks through Rainbow Park on the corner of Seventh and Cherry. It's an urban park, not in the best neighborhood; there's trash on the sidewalks that surround it and stores with boarded-up windows, and the bums and the down-and-outers who like to stand on the corners, panhandle for change and food. Whenever Georgie remembers, he stops at the Carl's Jr. up the street and buys Western Bacon Cheeseburgers, chicken strips, and criss-cut fries that he hands out to homeless who line the street, and whenever he has the time, he picks up at least two pieces of trash to throw away. Sometimes he buys Kentucky Fried Chicken instead of Carl's Junior, and sometimes he picks up three pieces of trash instead of two. He likes to pick up trash because it makes him feel like an environmentalist, like he's contributing in some way. Once, by mistake, he picked up a baby's soiled diaper, and it grossed him out so bad, he couldn't pick up trash for a month. Across the street from the park is the 7-11 and kitty corner is the Shell station, where Georgie buys his blue raspberry Slush Puppie, the best drink he's ever had in his life. It tastes like frozen cherry Kool-Aid, except it's carbonated slightly. Georgie drinks his Slush Puppie, and better than any orgasm, any bright sunny day, otherwise, he could be in heaven; the original Slush Puppie is that good, ever since he can remember.

Georgie feels good. It's a Wednesday, and he likes Wednesdays because that's when he sees Dr. C, same as Ben—

3:30 to 4:30. He likes Dr. C; he thinks she's kind, and he likes that she sees him (and Ben) on the half hour. It's different, it makes Georgie feel special, noticed.

Georgie knows that Dr. C doesn't believe he exists, that he's only a figment of Ben's imagination, or worse, a symptom of his pathology, but that's okay, Georgie doesn't mind. He knows he's real, and that's all that matters, at least for Georgie.

And Georgie knows all about Ben even if Ben doesn't know all about Georgie. Georgie knows how Ben thinks of nothing but Heidi but puts it on Georgie, says it's Georgie the character, Georgie the literary device (what a joke—being nothing but a literary device) who can't get over Claudia. Georgie knows better. It's Ben who can't get over Claudia.

Ben, when he thinks of the real Georgie at all, thinks of Georgie from the past, remembers Georgie in sex class, in the tree house. He doesn't think of Georgie in the present, the one who buys the DVDs on female masturbation, who works at understanding a woman's body, who sometimes wants nothing more than his partner's orgasm.

Ben dismisses Georgie, which sometimes hurts Georgie's feelings, but not today. Not when the sun is shining and the breeze is cool and Georgie gets to see Dr. C—he checks his watch—in another two hours.

He takes a seat on the bench nearest the swings, where he always sits, and watches a young mother push a little blond-haired boy, maybe three or four, higher and higher into the air, the little boy screaming in delight.

The problem, the all-consuming sadness and despair, for Georgie (Ben, too) stems, he knows, from his own mother. A woman Georgie's memory can't access. Ben has him locked out. Nobody gets to know Ben's mother. Nobody.

#

Georgie's ultimate goal is to be like Mozart on his deathbed with Salieri reminding him that he's a genius and will finish off works of his life, slowly dissolving in his insanity.

Georgie Bartholemew Gust: Might he rest in peace.[58]

---

[58] "Nothing else?" nudges Dr. C. I say, "Nothing. He's a loser. That's

why I created him, to infuse him with all my failures." Dr. C folds her legs, there's still plenty of time left in our session. I uncross my legs and look her in the eyes." The jogger, even in the springtime, he'd have on the same clothes, but they seemed to be getting raggedy, this spring. I began to tell Dr. C more about him, but nothing really new was added to this character I'd been attempting to develop for Dr. C to do something with.

52. SUPPORT THIS TROUPE

"So what do you want to talk about today, Ben?" asks Dr. C.

I say nothing. The two of us are alone in the room for now.

"You look . . . sad . . . today?"

I shrug.

"Anything going on?" asks Dr. C.

I shake my head.

Silence.

Georgie appears through my light tears. "Tell her," he says, "tell her."

The clock ticks.

I decide to say something. "Well, did I tell you about the jogger?"

Georgie shoots darts in my eyes. "Not him."

Dr. C nods. "The one who ran every day—Christmas, New Year's, it didn't matter—and who wore the same clothes no matter what the weather?"

Georgie sinks back into despair.

I nod 'yes.'

Dr. C asks, "What about him?"

"Nothing about him," Georgie interrupts. Dr. C doesn't hear anything. There's more silence. Silence. Silence. But Georgie wouldn't let the hour be filled with silence; this is just too awful.

"Did you want to talk about the jogger?" Dr. C nudges.

"Not really," I say. There's a long pause, until "I always thought he was doing my mother."

"That he was her lover?"

"No, Doc, just doing her."

"That's interesting."

"Not really."

Georgie wants to scream: Ask her, Why? Why is it interesting?

I shift in my chair, cross, uncross my legs, and ask, "Why?"

Dr. C's eyebrows rise just slightly. "Why is it interesting?"

I nod 'yes.'

Dr. C hesitates.

Silence. The silences are killing Georgie. Make them stop.

"Well," says Dr. C, "if I'm remembering correctly, didn't you tell me that the jogger was young? A college student, I think you said."

I nod. 'So what?'

"Well, thinking about her age at the time," explains Dr. C, "that would have made him young enough to be her son?"

I nod again.

"And didn't you tell me that he ran silently? That nobody in the neighborhood even knew his name?"

I nod. "I called him Mr. Clean."

Dr. C's face pales out. "That's interesting to me."

"Mr. Clean?" I ask.

She swallows a toad: "No, Ben, the whole thing."

53. DEMONS

There are demons in Ben's bedroom, demons that make his dresser crackle and pop.

He lies alone in his bed, in his bedroom, beneath the silver-and-brown-brocade bedspread and wonders how long he has before the demons take over completely. When he first moved in, they played only in the living room, then in his office, making his computer shut down, start up in the middle of the night. Ben would be lying in bed, trying to sleep and the chime of Windows starting up, shutting down would wake him up. It got so he finally unplugged the computer before going to sleep, and that should have taken care of the problem, but it didn't; the computer still came on, shut down.

Then the demons moved to the bathroom, made the lights flash, the shower run. Some people—not Ben, not Georgie—would have taken all the activity as a sign, an excuse to move. All Ben did, all Ben could do, was buy crystals and sage from the psychic shop down the street, look online for an exorcist.

Finally got one: Reverend Constanza who drove up from La Jolla, took one look at how Ben lived and tripled the price. So Ben spent $3000 for Reverend Constanza to sprinkle sage around the baseboards, place crystals in the northeast corners of all the rooms, and tell Ben that he needed his aura cleansed. For another $3000. Wouldn't have happened if he lived in a two-floor walk-up over on Seventh. But living where he did—overlooking the Pacific—Reverend Constanza thought she could take him, jack up the price, feed his paranoia. Still made Ben mad. Especially since, if anything, the demons were even worse.

Ben lies in bed, watches the fan above his bed turn on, turn off, listens to the TV sputter as if electricity were running through it. *It wouldn't be so bad,* Ben thinks, *if he weren't so alone, so goddamn fucking alone, day in, day out.* Not like Georgie, who's out every night with another woman.

Georgie, it seems, is dedicated to getting over Claudia. Georgie lately is absolutely manic about overcoming Claudia. Not Ben. Ben can't do much of anything but lie in bed in the middle of the night and listen to the demons who've overtaken his world.

Or at least his electronics.

54. GEORGIE AND DR. C

Only Georgie shows up at Dr. C's. He is frantic, paces, can't sit still. He's going out of his mind, crawling out of his skin. Dr. C watches him. Georgie can't stand to be watched. He avoids her eyes, swallows continuously, sniffs, tics, hops. "You look agitated," she tells him.

"Agitated?" He looks like he's from another world, that's how he looks.

"Can you sit?" she asks.

Georgie, because he's so passive, so submissive, sits down immediately, pops back up. "No," he says. "I can't."

Dr. C smiles. "What's going on?"

"Going on? Nothing's going on. Everything's going on. How can I answer that? I can't. I can't decide. I can't decide what *is* going on, what *isn't* going on. I can't fucking decide. Don't ask me."

Silence. The silences fucking kill Georgie, make his head throb. He needs a temple massage; someone to touch him, to love him. Not like all the women—how many have there been— sucking his dick, his balls, his ass, fucking him. Someone real who loves him. Someone who can see beyond what he pretends to be and touch his soul. That's what he needs. That's what he'll never have. The thought, the realization, spirals him downward. He thinks of his meds. At home. Swallowing pill after pill, bottle after bottle.

Peace. He needs peace.

55. MOTHER GHOST

Ben shares his bedroom with demons; the lights flicker; the TV goes on and off, on and off. He can't take it. His mother/his angel/his older woman comes to him, pushes the hair off his forehead, strokes his hand. "You need to move, Baby," she says.

Ben groans, rolls to his side. "I'm not going anywhere."

The older woman climbs into bed with him, strokes his back, tickles him. "You need to move, Baby."

Ben climbs out of bed.

The older woman—his mother, his angel, his lover—is an illusion. Not real. The voices in his head—her voice, so soothing, so insistent—aren't real.

He brushes his teeth, notes his reflection in the mirror. His hair is dirty, and he could use a shave. He ducks his head, spits into the sink, straightens. His angel, his mother, his lover is behind him smiling into the mirror at him.

"This house isn't good for you, Baby," she says.

How's he supposed to listen to an illusion? Better to listen to his Perplexity. He ignores her.

She pokes the back of his head. Hard. Tells him: "I am not an illusion."

He continues to ignore her.

"You're not going to be able to ignore me forever," she says.

Maybe not forever, Ben thinks, *but for as long as I need to.*

"And how long's that going to be?" his illusion asks.

How in the hell is he supposed to get the voices out of his head when they can read his every thought?

"Not every voice," she says. "Just me. And trust me, BJ, you need to move out of this house." She pauses for dramatic effect. "It's haunted."

He knew it. He knew it all along. The fucking place was haunted.

"With demons?" he asks.

"With memories," she tells him.

He'd rather have demons.

"Who wouldn't?" she says. "Memories are much harder to get rid of."

Ben ticks, bobbing his head to the right then the left then forward, raises his right eyebrow and grimaces.

"Don't like memories, do you, Baby?"

"Illusion. Illusion," he screams silently. "Not real."

Still ticking, he heads into the kitchen for a Red Bull; his illusion follows right behind, tsk-tsking the entire way.

"Caffeine," she says, "is the absolute worst thing for ticking."

"I know that," Ben says, sniffing. Sniffing so hard he worries for a second that his brains will leak right out his ears.

"Stupid, stupid, stupid," his illusion says.

"Shut up," Ben tells her.

But she ignores him. "First," she says, "you don't have brains. You have a brain. And it won't leak out your ears from sniffing. The only way it'll leak out is if you decide to shoot yourself in the head, then it'll leak. Out your ears. Out your nose. Want to try?"

His illusion is crazier than he is. Figures. John Nash gets a CIA operative for his illusion; Ben gets a cross between Carol Kane and Sandra Bernhardt, neither of whom appeal to him and neither of whom are the least bit stable.

His illusion, dressed in white gossamer, appears directly in front of him.

She clears her throat. "What I said," she says, "is, would you like to try?"

Okay, okay, okay, he knows she's an illusion—not real. He's on dangerous ground. The more you talk to an illusion, a hallucination the stronger they get, and still he can't help himself. The words are out of his mouth before he's had a chance to think.

"Try what?"

His illusion/his gossamer angel hands him a blue steel, white grip .38. "Blowing your head off," she says. "Watching your brain leak out your nose and ears. Want to? Want to try?"

She presses the gun into his hands.

"Nobody'll know," she says. "You're all alone. Who's to know?"

She's the devil, a demon. Ben backs up, letting the gun slip to the floor. His angel/demon/mother retrieves it, presses it again into his hands, and smiles.

244

Funny how he never noticed her teeth—yellow and snaggled, sharp. Her teeth scare him. He shudders, fighting the urge to hop. First on his left foot then on his right. First left then right. Like reading. Left to right. Left to right. He's going to hop; he's going to tic.

The teeth, the breath—they're his mother's—lipstick smeared on the enamel. She scares him. She's always scared him.

He wants to go home; he is home. There's nowhere left to go. Why not? Why not pick up the gun? Wasn't it his mother who always said, "Benjy, you check out, remember: Check out fast. No drugs. No hanging yourself. You jump, Benj. From the thirty-second floor. You'll never live to tell about it."

Then she laughs. Cackles. His mother was a witch. Long, pointed fingers. Nails filed sharp. Always grabbing at him, digging into his flesh. Is she dead? Lord, Hear My Prayer. Kill her. Kill her so I don't have to.

His mother: The Hamptons. 1987. Ben is eleven. His mother is heavy that year—250 pounds at least—wears a massive, red-striped bathing suit with white, gossamer cover-up. She floats, bounces, galumphs into his bedroom, night after night, crying.

"You don't know what it's like, Benjy. You don't know what it's like."

He loves his mother, doesn't want to see her cry. He'll do whatever she needs to get her to stop.

He sits up, the blankets slipping from his skinny, naked eleven-year-old chest. His mother's at the end of the bed, sobbing.

"He's leaving me, Benjy. He's leaving me."

"Mom, don't cry. Please don't cry. Please."

His mother. She buries her head in her hands, sobs, her giant bosom heaving. Ben watches, watches the sleeves of her nightgown slip off her shoulders, exposing the top of her breast, the massive brown areola. He doesn't know what to do. He's never seen his mother's breasts. He wants her to cover them back up, but she's crying. She won't stop.

"What'll I do, Benjy? Where will I go?"

He hates to hear his mother cry. It's worse than hearing his sister cry, almost as bad as hearing his father cry. Mothers shouldn't cry. They should be happy.

"He's the only man I ever loved, Benjy. What am I going to do?"

Ben doesn't know what she's going to do; he just wishes she'd cover her breasts back up. He doesn't want to see them. He shouldn't have to see them. They're gross and too big. And scary. His mother's breasts are scary.

"And the only man who ever touched me. Oh, Benjy."

Ben thinks about his father touching his mother, thinks about those porn mags and all those pussies—those wide open pussies—and his father touching his mother. There. His father fucking his mother. There. It's gross, Ben knows it's gross, but he's still getting a hard-on; he can feel it tenting his pajama bottoms. He wishes his mother would leave.

Instead, she flops to her stomach across the bed, her hand resting on Ben's thigh. Her fingers are cold, her nails sharp. Ben can feel them tattooing his skin, working their way up to his groin, massaging, moving inward to his balls, to his dick, the shaft.

Ben tries to move away, but his mother's hand holds him tight, begins to stroke him.

"Your father," she says, "was the only man who ever touched me."

Her voice drops. "Sexually, I mean."

Ben wants his mother to stop, but he's paralyzed; he can't talk, can't move. Even when she moves up his body, even when his mother's naked breasts smash against his bare chest, even when she kisses his neck, drags her tongue across his skin, down his chest to his belly to his cock, even when she takes him in her mouth begins sucking on him, even when he comes with a shudder that overtakes his entire body, leaving him ashamed and humiliated, wishing he were dead, even then Ben can't say a word, can't move a muscle. He is dead. Invisible. Floating high above the world, watching his mother cough discreetly into her hand depositing the prepubescent cum she's sucked from him onto her fingers.

"Oh, my," she says, tugging the straps of her nightgown back over her shoulders. "Oh my."

And Ben, still floating high above the world, doesn't know why she's saying that, why she's repeating it, why she won't leave, go back to her own room.

She slides off the bed, readjusts her nightgown, flips her hair behind her ears. "Benjy," she says, "what we did right now, I don't want you thinking there was anything wrong with that. I was just giving you a bit of relief. Okay, honey?"

Still Ben can't talk.

"The thing is though . . ." his mother stops, bites her lips, lowers her brow, searching, Ben thinks, for just the right word. His mother's like that—obsessive about finding exactly the right word.

"So, okay," she finally says. "The thing is some people— your dad included—don't always understand how things are between mothers and sons, so I'm not saying don't tell anyone, I'm just saying you should probably be kind of careful about who you do tell, because I know you, Benjy, and I know how you never want anyone to . . . disapprove of you."

His mother waits, then adds, "Or be mad at you."

Ben says nothing, his stomach in knots, remembering how that feels—when nobody's happy with him.

"Or not even talk to you anymore."

Ben can't take it; he starts crying.

"For God's sakes, Benjy, lighten up," his mother says, then takes his nose between her fingers and twists.

Ben's tears fall harder.

His mother, her nightgown slipping from her shoulder again, bounces out of the room.

"Lighten up, Baby. Life's just too fuckin' short to go through it all hangdog. Know what I'm saying?"

And then she's gone, and the room is quiet and Ben thinks about her, about his mother, and how she goes to every single one of his Little League games and how she bakes brownies from scratch, makes sundaes out of them with Breyer's vanilla ice cream and hot fudge sauce. He remembers his ninth birthday and his mother taking him and three of his friends to McDonald's and then over to Coney Island even though she said nothin' but niggers and spics ever went to Coney Island *these days*. He remembers his mother, how she bandages his knees when he falls, slathers them with Bactyne, then kisses them—her mouth open to suck out the germs—then sticks colored Band-Aids all over them. He has a good mother, Ben thinks. A mother who loves him, who takes good care of him, doesn't smack him around like Luke's mother. Ben's lucky: He has a mother who loves him.

He falls asleep thinking about his mother loving him and his father leaving.

56. DR. C'S OFFICE: GEORGIE AND BEN

Dr. C notices a change in Ben: "You look . . . different. Has something come up?"

Ben paces around the office. Everything seems rushed and urgent.

"No," he says. "Nothing's come up. That's not what I'd say."

Ben can't talk, can't answer her. His face is flushed; his stomach's in knots. He paces more quickly.

Georgie says, "Sit down."

Dr. C says, "Would you like to sit, Ben."

Ben sits, feels like he's going to faint, puts his head between his legs. Georgie strokes his hair.

Dr. C asks, "What is it, Ben?"

Ben shakes his head. Georgie leaves his hand on Ben's head, willing Ben to feel his strength. His love.

Georgie pushes Ben. "You can tell her."

Ben shakes his head. "Dr. C's part of the conspiracy."

Georgie says, "There's no conspiracy."

Ben doesn't move.

Dr. C asks, "Can we talk about it, Ben?"

Georgie pushes Ben to his feet, makes Ben drag his chair across the room to Dr. C's chair.

"She's okay, Ben. She wants to help," says Georgie.

Ben looks up. "I remembered something last night."

Dr. C looks at him. "Yes?"

Ben shrugs. "It probably wasn't anything, you know."

"What did you remember?" asks Dr. C.

Ben sits back. "Nothing."

"Ben?" nudges Dr. C.

Georgie says to Ben, "She's okay, Ben. She likes you."

Ben replies silently to Georgie, "No, she doesn't."

Ben asks Dr. C, "Do you like me?"

Dr. C says, "Of course, I like you, Ben. You're my client."

Ben shakes his head. "No. As a person. Do you like me as a person? Like if we were out in public, would you want to be my friend?"

Dr. C folds her legs. "I don't know, Ben. Not for sure. But probably. I know I like you in here, in the office."

Ben waits for more.

Dr. C continues. "You're a very smart man, Ben. I like smart men. And you're a very kind man. Very articulate. These are all traits I enjoy in a man. In a friend."

Ben still waits for more.

Dr. C continues. "So, I think, yes, Ben, I'd probably want to be your friend."

Georgie urges Ben. "Isn't that enough?"

Ben says to Dr. C, "It was about my mother."

"What you remembered?" she asks.

Ben nods. "At first, I thought it was the demons again. I told you about the demons?"

Dr. C nods yes.

". . . And the illusion? The woman. I told you about her? She looks kind of like Carol Kane or Sandra Bernhardt? Do you remember?"

Dr. C nods again. "You said it was just your luck to have a hallucination look like a cross between the only two women in the world that you find repugnant."

"You did listen," Ben says.

"I always listen," Dr. C replies.

Ben smiles. "Last night I had a realization. I realized that my Illusion actually looks a lot like my mother."

Dr. C's eyebrows go up.

". . . At least last night, she did. Last night she looked fat. Like my mother." He pauses. "Like my mother when I was eleven."

"That was the year your father left?"

Ben looks away, nods slightly. "The year I was diagnosed with Tourette's." He pauses. "My mother said I twitched."

Dr. C lets him continue. "She said I wet the bed."

"Did you?"

Ben shrugs. "I don't remember. Maybe." He pauses. "But last night, what I realized was that my Illusion really is a demon. Not like one you see in Hollywood movies or shit like that but the kind of demon that can send you right to hell. You know what I mean?"

250

Dr. C leans in. "Why don't you tell me?"

"Okay. Hell on earth, that's what I'm talking about. That's what I've been talking about all the time."

"Like your metaphor?"

Ben nods. "She's not a demon; she's my memory. She's the person who put me in hell."

"Your mother?" Dr. C asks.

Ben nods, looks down at the ground, tears welling up in his eyes.

"What'd she do, Ben?"

He shakes his head. He can't tell. Dr. C'll go away if he tells, she'll think he's crazy, not worth anything.

Georgie strokes Ben's head, puts his finger beneath Ben's chin, tilts it upward.

Dr. C imposes. "Did she hurt you, Ben?"

Georgie says for Ben, "She raped me. I mean that's not what she would have called it, but that's what it was. Like all those dykes and women libber bitches say: If she can't say 'no,' then it's rape. And I couldn't say 'no.'"

"To the sex?" asks Dr. C.

Ben, to himself, says, "That's what it was. It was rape." He lifts his head on his own accord. "She did. She raped me. My mother. She went down on me; she jerked me off. Private lessons, she called it, said I was lucky, that it wasn't many sons whose mothers made time for them like that, who taught them what a real woman wanted, needed." Ben shudders, fighting tears. "The only thing she wouldn't do was intercourse. She didn't want her son getting her pregnant ..."

Ben laughs bitterly.

". . . Said she couldn't run the risk of giving birth to anyone more screwed up than me."

Dr. C rises, crosses the room to sit next to Ben. She takes him in her arms as he cries hard, for the last time, draining his soul, pouring all that he'd pent up inside, the downpour of heavy tears; his identity was about to bloom.

"Cry, it's time, Ben, let it out," Christine said, "let it out," as she breathed into her own sacred pain, her shrink-wrapped eyes welled up with the genuine and pure agony she could no longer contain, for all that she was losing.

Things would never be the same; they say relationships like this never last.

Judgments aside, the living, colorful beauty was remarkable.

57. TO THE SHORE

Downstairs, somewhere back in Long Beach, Dr. C stands outside the front door, watching a taxi pull away, noting with a sigh that she had just missed it.

Her eyes focus farther, as a telescope would, and she sees that she has succeeded. That Ben or Georgie has succeeded. She smiles. The passenger in the back seat wears an oversized black hat with a pom-pom on top. Dr. C remembers day one, but in a wholly different light now.

Like I said earlier that I would wonder . . . I wondered and wondered.

The cleaning crew would have been here any minute as I lay holding my Living, Colorful Beauty, letting go; the memories of my life would be lost and forgotten otherwise.

#

Regardless of anybody, regardless of Claudia or Kelly or Moms or Pops, and regardless of the musing Gladice, or rather the muse of Claudia, the muse she's been for me . . . I still sit here in the house, here in New Mexico, and concern myself with my own death.

Enya's beautiful sagas of song, alternative song, resonate through the room I've situated myself in, inside, here in this room that has been turned into my mindful awareness of self. It has "me" written all over it. Semen on the cement walls, like a dirty old motel room, fucking cinderblock and vaginal membranes from some psych ward panties I collected from some slut, some crazy bitch. Aside from that . . .

58. LIVING, COLORFUL BEAUTY

On 10/31/07, <Kelly.Nolan > wrote:

Honey,

You are the sweetest man alive, and I thank god every day that you have come into my life.

Thank you for the flowers, the orchids, the bonsai tree, and the ficus. They are so alive—like our relationship.

I love you very very much. -Kelly

#

Kelly,

I want to hold your hand, even if it's just for the one second that you'd want to hold it. If you don't give up on me, then I hope that you'll just do nothing different, except just to help me realize just how bad I am, because I need to really surrender to that. Please swallow me up, break me in your frustrating rages, but give me something I can hold on to with some kind of reason and meaning. I can't bear to see the ill effects that I've bestowed on you. I see me in you, and I can't stand it.

What should I do?

Should I let myself die, Kelly? I don't want to die.

Love,

Ben

#

. . . I just wrote you a letter: It's real garbage, Kelly; just an attempt to write you a letter, but it came across real bitter and angry—I meant it to be genuine and friendly, but once again it focuses on the negatives and my self and my giving up, so to speak—my possessing you.—It lets you know that I inherently want to be left alone to rot it out (Rotting It Out: sorry, good new title for Living, Colorful Beauty). That I can't stand that I see myself in you—it's ugly and scary.

I've left the letter on the kitchen counter along with your mail and mine (plus diabetes prescriptions from Dr. C), my poster from mail-order (you may open it for a look—it's small, but it's a good quality, frame-able poster that just says kind how I'm feeling lately: FUCK YOU, YOU FUCKING FUCK). The new paper (100 sheets) is on your desk, and my new T-shirts are hanging in my bedroom closet closest to the entry, in case you were interested. I don't like the "I haven't escaped, they gave me a day pass" one (I'll keep it for the house). But see if you can read, if you feel up to it, what the one says that's aqua blue with the psychedelic insignia on it. It says *Fuck You,* kind of in code. Sorry, don't take it personally. It's *my* stuff.

I'm still angry and have little energy left.

I meant what I said in the letter about distance and my inferiority. I am losing myself and losing you—for this is not closeness we're getting involved in; it's my faults we're getting involved in. And I am killing you, more than I could ever kill myself. I just can't help it so far; you must be a wreck. My letter was meant to be apologetic, to acknowledge my regression and my false sense of worth—call it depression—I'm not saying it's worse than that.

It's the caboose of these personalities, these identities, the reactions of others, and this philosophy, that just shrank up to fill me earlier in life than they did for most people, who'll live to an older age than I might; once the train runs along the tracks, the caboose moves forward, but always looking back (like in my journals from the Claudia intermission— "R.L.B." - *Reader, Looking Back* . . .). It doesn't serve as anything that contributes any power, like the engine in the front; the caboose is not entirely necessary, and surely it stays at the tail end of the society hanging out with the freight, the body, with the cars that make up the majority or essence of the train.

You could jump off, and nobody would notice, or really care, as life goes on . . . the train will by itself and together, stop-and-go, and hold itself together, and function . . .

Have energy and eventually die.

#

Dearest Ben,

256

There's absolutely no reason to apologize for anything. I think you're pretty awesome. You're the hugest and most adored part of me that I can imagine.

—Kelly.

#

I think about the kids in Paris, from a long time ago, and my sweat starts to disappear. And I don't itch anymore. My skin has cleared up a bit, and I feel a flash of heat on my face, like the sun hit me; I can feel my blood flow. I'm not entirely invisible. Not entirely finished yet . . . I feel like maybe something's happening.

59. BACK TO THE HEAT

Dear Kelly,

So sorry in advance for coming across as bitter—you'll see why after a few minutes' reading—but looking over your critique, well, haven't I left enough room in this novel for any readers' interpretations? Who is my reader? And didn't I leave any place for the readers of my greatest work to date—this one—to come up with judgments, images, or even any emotions of their own? have I simply 'chosen' certain fragments of this anguished life—and, yes, done a real good job of getting into the depressing, yet fascinating, train-wreck mentalities of both Georgie and myself? But is that all I've done? Is that all I can do? I guess so. I'm pretty sure about that.

I question this work now.

The whimper, the bang—it's not really over yet, is it? Tell me it's not over yet!

And that . . . you've done "Gotta keep at it," right?

You're telling me I should keep combing the hair out of this piece, that again it's 'not good enough,' but I've got to spend another year polishing and writing and working on new additions, alas . . . I know that I haven't even put any provocative scenery, much less incorporated any 'real' action and dialogue, or any depth—I know, yay! Praise the Lord for no depth, by the way—might you have any empathy in a year for the characters in my life, as part of the Living, Colorful Beauty—you are my living colorful beauty, but as you read this, can't you feel anything more than, 'oh, okay, I see, another Chuck Palahniuk wanna-be, ooh it's the next Bukowski, or fucking Kathy Acker—I love her!' Am I just some creative writer whose ramblings resonate? In your crotch? In your heart? . . . And to call this book . . . (I'm sorry, something happened yesterday, and I'm hurt and . . . um . . . spent . . .) you call this novel, if that's what it is, "unfinished business?" What is this? You think that I, as the writer, the narcissist, the fucking cupcake lover . . . whatever the hell I am—you say I'm someone who just has lots of imagination and a witty eye for detail, experimental structure, and . . . peace? (This is my stepmother . . . This is sex with a condom . . . This is

Vanilla Sky with Tom Cruise, *this is fucking tops, baby!)* This stuff is about hope, I thought . . . for everything that was unclear before, the hope that things would come to fruition, becoming real, tangible, loving, peaceful . . . things, like us . . . Like we want to be . . . Like, who we are—or without hope, so what? Okay, you want to get all edit-y on me, well here. (I'm sorry, baby . . . I'm trying to get to the point. Please bear with me here . . .) Here is another non sequitur: Our fucking dogs are fucking barking again at the demons in the fucking house, need to fucking soundproof the freaking office here. Okay, I've had enough. I'm really trying to be level-headed and . . . nice here. It's nice, okay, Kelly-baby?

#

Remember the tapes from Gladice—the kiddie porn stuff I starred in as a kid? Okay? This is your brain on drugs-like. This is what I found in my frustrating venture out there into the outside world, all on my own, yesterday when I walked all alone, all the way to our usual psychic advisor, the one who we've been seeing since we've lived out here in the desert together. And this is nothing about those silly tapes. (The psychic, so the readers know, was Sabrina—but Sabrina wasn't there, so Sister Clara was filling in for her, she was down the street at the New Age Shoppe as usual, but I wasn't prepared for anything unusual to would follow me there.)

And just so you know, Kelly, I do love you, you Lady to love, and I want you; I want you so badly. Do I have you, Kelly? Kelly, I know we are both still new at all this. And I admit to my obsession and that I'm dependent on you, just as I'm dependent on my fucking family—they're still staring at me. But I'm happy, you see? Because Sister Clara—whom I don't think you remember from the meditations we go to—she was there at the first night, I think, the first night we attended them, about three weeks ago, and we met that massage therapist who said she could help with the Tourette's stuff—we never followed through with her. Anyway, Clara was sort of off to the side with the Shoppe owner, Evelen.

Clara—she's probably in her early fifties—had that straight, shoulder-length, gray hair, a huge Celtic cross pendant, and

Southwestern New Age style, you know, a poncho and pagan shoes with huge buckles. Silver and stone rings galore on unpainted fingers, nails kind of like yours, a little long and natural-looking? Do you remember her? Do you remember Clara?

So I step inside, asking for Sabrina; I'm extremely out of breath, as the long walk to the Shoppe was tiring—what is it, a mile or so? The Shoppe-keepers ask if I'm all right, because I'm strangely red-faced and unsure of myself. Though I tell them it's my allergies, I don't think that's really true. The Shoppe women and the owner, specifically, they look rather inquisitive— strangely so—and they ask where you are and I tell them that you're home working on your own book, as you are, and I add that you're excited because it looks like you'll probably be showcased in the *New Yorker* in a few months. One by one, the Shoppe-keepers inform me that Clara—who we both barely know, or at least I barely know her—Sister Clara wants to see me in private. I feel a sense of disillusionment.

The owner, Evelyn—that larger, older lady who always talks about her son—she escorts me to the back room and into one of the smaller psychic chambers off to the side, and Clara is seated before me. I sit down before her. I'm totally wondering what's happening, so I ask her, "Clara? What's happening?"

Clara continues to remove a tiny Mead spiral binder from a small paper bag to her side, lying on the flimsy, cloth-covered reading table between us. She says, "Ben, to put it simply, I was in the middle of a meditation and I am aware that we've never really even been properly introduced, but I started writing down, drawing what I was seeing. And I couldn't bear to let this go by without witness."

"Really?" I said, still not impressed by anything yet, until she opened the first page of her little red notebook.

Clara said, "You know who came into my meditation, whose soul came into my meditation?"

I guessed, "Kelly?"

"Kelly? No."

"Then who?" I asked, a little concerned at this point.

She took a long breath and said, "You did, Ben."

She showed me what she'd seen, what came to her, as it was carefully penciled in her notebook. At this point, I was both completely thunderstruck and crestfallen. And those are fucking great words, might I add; I nearly peed my pants. You gotta hear this!

Now Clara knew nothing of Georgie or of Claudia, much less about you or even me—before yesterday—but she started to comment on each of her pencil drawings as if she knew everything. Yes, *everything*!

Clara said, as if she was without a hint of doubt, "This is you, Ben. *Not* Georgie. This is you and your mother, your *real* mother, not your stepmother; your biological mother, Rose." And I could see what Clara had drawn: a precious little boy, I mean an infant boy . . . with a little penis, too! And the mother was holding the little boy, me, the baby, by the dick—and only by the fucking dick. This woman, my own mother, was torturing me. *How* could *I remember this? What the fuck,* I thought. And Clara started flipping the filled-in pages—a whole notebook of sick and demented art—of me and my mother and then me together with my stepmother and then my father and then my teachers from what appeared to be nursery school, even the nanny from Trinidad who was supposed to be taking care of me. Separately, they're all performing very disturbing acts of violence and aggression on my innocent infantile genitals. In one of them, a nurse of some kind, who appeared to have the same skin tone as the nanny, was performing medical procedures on my skin, in the private areas, healing, stitching up, and bandaging my bottom and my little baby cock. Clara explains, "This was so that you wouldn't know later on in your lifetime; you might have a subconscious memory now and then, that's all."

Sister Clara hands the book to me, and I leave without a word. I'm sobbing. I'm back on the road, back on my way home again. I have this book now in my very own hands, and I can, strangely, somehow manage to breathe, really breathe. Ahhh. You should see this fucking thing, Kelly. This is why I can't function like a normal human being—this is what they meant, Sabrina and some of the other psychics we've seen, when they've implied that there appeared to be some 'stuff' that harmed me before I could actually remember.

I don't even know if what I have down below is in fact a natural penis. I'm crying so hard now; I kick away the dirt at my feet, but I can't kick it good enough.

I'm almost home. I have only whatever dignity I *am*, whatever *might* be, hopefully left inside. I am nothing *but* my self.

I am just and only that.

Move in with me, Kelly, I mean for the rest of our time together. In the next chapter, hastily, I have Georgie moving off to another place and I've put in a rather dull "Bang" finale— you'll see—it's a symbolic sort of ending, a painting of the walls . . . you'll see, not really any bang, might even want to delete it. But this shit from the Shoppe, from Clara, from the family, and so forth is something I could never even imagine, thinking I was just some lousy sex-addicted schizophrenic who had a bright imagination—so what—and an flair for vivid, you know, witty depthless scenes, short-film kind of stuff.

I can't love these people, can I, all these people I write about, really? Can I? That I live in a fantasy world full-time, so it seems, so that's what it is. So fucking what? I can only forgive them for all that they won't cop to. I won't call the cops, I'm thinking I need to write out a brand-new living will. I want you to live out the rest of my life with the family's fucking money— through my fucking cursed trust fund. No, I can't kill myself, too heartbreaking, and that wouldn't be fair, plus it would just create more anguish, and who needs that. Why don't you go and read fucking *Bridges of Madison County*, for God's sake. I am going to stay right here and wait for you to come back home. I thought you were already home by now, baby.

I know that we started out pretty rough, Kelly, and my family would never approve of us, but I'm waiting for you, baby. Like you said, the stuff we write and say does have its mysterious way of manifesting itself in the real world . . . I just want to live, and if that means having superficial relationships with family and friends, then so be it. Never thought this would end, and I'm sorry about that unending obsession with Claudia; at least now I have a little idea of why it was as it was.

I'm still sitting in the psych ward, in my home—the cinderblocks and cement and all—I haven't been able to escape here yet, but they give me day passes and things. At least I'm not alone. After all, they might really need that cause of death that the cameras around me will show, if they ever get to it.

We're all getting older and wiser. Sometimes you just have to listen to the sounds of your life. I can't see the sounds anymore, only the colors. And they're brilliant and alive.

As for this afternoon, I'm going to go out and get the groceries and the fertilizer for the lawn outside, and can't forget the firewood, finally. We can build a beautiful fire tonight— might I find the living colorful beauty inside me, inside us, for the memories nearly forgotten, I'll make the man I am today. It's okay, now. I hope—just gotta hold onto this. Might have found my self at last. We'll just have to see about that.

That's all I've got in me—all that I could get out. It's the best I could do, Kelly, Claudia, everyone . . .

Always,

Your Ben Forever . . .

The End

www.ingramcontent.com/pod-product-compliance
Lightning Source LLC
Chambersburg PA
CBHW061958280526
45787CB00005B/1917